The Building of Character

The Building of Character

By

J.R. Miller D.D.

Bottom of the Hill Publishing

Memphis, TN

www.BottomoftheHillPublishing.com

ISBN: 978-1-61203-167-5

"Build it well, whate'er you do;
Build it straight, and strong, and true;
Build it clear, and high, and broad:
Build it for the eye of God."

"By trifles in our common ways,
Our characters are slowly piled,
We lose not all our yesterdays;
The man has something of the child,
Part of the past to all the present cleaves,
As the rose-odors linger in the fading leaves.
"In ceaseless toil, from year to year,
Working with loath or willing hands,
Stone upon stone we shape, we rear,
Till the completed fabric stands.
And, when the last hush hath all labor stilled,
The searching fire will try what we have striven to build."

Forward

Nothing else we can do or make in this world is so important as that which we build along the years in ourselves. What we are at the end is a great deal truer test of living than what we have or what we have done.

It is hoped that these chapters may give helpful suggestions to thoughtful readers toward the attaining of the things in life which are more excellent. The author is exceedingly grateful to the many who have written him of the strength, comfort, encouragement, guidance, or inspiration received form his former books, and sends out this new volume in the hope that it, too, may have a ministry of helpfulness.

J.R. M.

Philadelphia.

Table of Contents

Chapter 1

The Building of Character

"Souls are built as temples are,—
Here a carving rich and quaint,
There the image of a saint;
Here a deep-hued pane to tell
Sacred truth or miracle.
Every little helps the much;
Every careful, careless touch
Adds a charm or leaves a scar."

The building of character is the most important business of life. It matters little what works a man may leave in the world; his real success is measured by what he has wrought along the years in his own being.

True character must be built after divine patterns. Every man's life is a plan of God. There is a divine purpose concerning it which we should realize. In the Scriptures we find the patterns for all the parts of the character, not only for its great and prominent elements, but also for its most minute features, — the delicate lines and shadings of its ornamentation. The commandments, the beatitudes, all Christ's precepts, the ethical teachings of the apostles, all show us the pattern after which we are to fashion our character.

It is a great thing for us to have a lofty thought of life, and ever to seek to reach it. Said Michael Angelo: "Nothing makes the soul so pure, so religious, as the endeavor to create something perfect; for God is perfection, and whosoever strives for it, strives for something that is godlike." The seeking itself makes us nobler, holier, purer, stronger. We grow ever toward that for which we long. Many searches are unrewarded. Men seek for gold, and do not find it. They try to attain happiness, but the vision ever recedes as they press toward it. The quest for true nobleness is one that is rewarded. "Blessed are they which do hunger and thirst after righteousness; For they shall be filled," is our Lord's own word. Longing for spiritual good shall never be in vain

"The thing we long for, that we are
For one transcendent moment;"

And unceasing longing, with earnest reaching after the good, little lifts the life into the permanent realization of that which is thus persistently sought.

There are certain things essential in all building. Every structure requires a good foundation. Without this it never can rise into real strength and grandeur. The most beautiful building reared on sand is insecure and must fall. There is only one foundation for Christian character. We must build on the rock; that is, we must have, as the basis of our character, great, eternal principles.

One of these principles is truth. Ruskin tells us that in a famous Italian cathedral there are a number of colossal figures high up among the heavy timbers that support the roof. From the pavement, these statues have appearance of great beauty. Curious to examine them, Ruskin says he climbed one day to the roof, and stood close beside them. Bitter was his disappointment to find that only the parts of the figures which could be seen from the pavement were carefully finished. The hidden side was rough and undressed.

It is not enough to make our lives true only so far as men can see them. We have but scorn for men who profess truth, and then in their secret life reveal falsehood, deception, insincerity. There must be truth through and through in the really noble and worthy building. A little flaw, made by a bubble of air in the casting, has been the cause of the breaking of the great beam years afterward, and the falling of the immense bridge whose weight rested upon it. Truth must be in the character, — absolute truth. The least falsehood mars the beauty of the life.

Another of these essential principles is purity. "Whatsoever thing are pure," says the apostle in the same breath with whatsoever things are true, and just, and honorable. It is a canon of art, that an artist who lives badly never can paint a good picture; nor can a man who lives badly ever build up a really beautiful character. Only he who has a pure heart can see God, to know what life's ideal is. Only he whose hands are clean can build after the perfect pattern.

Love is another quality which must be wrought into this foundation. Love is the reverse of selfishness. It is the holding of all the life as Christ's, to be used to bless others "So long as I have been here," said President Lincoln, after his second election, "I have not willingly planted a thorn in any man's bosom." That is one phase of love, — never needlessly to give pain or do hurt to a fellow-being. The other part is the positive, — to live to do the greatest good to every other being whenever opportunity offers.

> "Do any hearts beat faster,
> Do any faces brighten,
> To hear your footsteps on the stair,
> To meet you, greet you, anywhere?
> Are you so like you Master,
> Dark shadows to enlighten?
> Are any happier to-day
> Through words they have heard you say?
> Life were not worth the living
> If no one were the better
> For having met you on the way,
> And known the sunshine of your stay."

Truth, purity, love, — these are example of the immutable principles which must be built into the foundation of the temple of character. We never can have a noble structure without a strong and secure foundation.

On the foundation thus laid the character must be build. No magnificent building ever grew up by miracle. Stone by stone it rose, each block laid in its place by toil and effort. "You cannot dream yourself into a character," says a writer; "you must hammer and forge yourself one." Even with the best foundation there must be faithful, patient building unto the end.

Then each one must build his own character. No one can do it for him. No one but yourself can make your life beautiful. No one can be true, pure, honorable, and loving for you. A mother's prayers and teachings cannot give you strength of soul and grandeur of spirit. We are taught to edify one another, and we do, indeed, help to build up each other's life-temple. Consciously or unconsciously, we are continually leaving touches on the souls of others, — touches of beauty or of marring. In every book we read the author lays something new on the wall of our life. Every hour's companionship with another gives either a touch of beauty, or a stain to our spirit. Every song that is sung in our ear enters into our heart and becomes part of our being. Even the natural scenery amid which we dwell leaves its impression upon us. Thus others, thus all things about us, do indeed have their place as builders of our character.

But we are ourselves the real builders. Others may lift the blocks into place, but we must lay them on the wall. Our own hands give the touches of beauty or of blemish, whatever hands of others hold the brushes or mix the colors for us. If the building is marred or unsightly when it is finished, we cannot say it was some other one's fault. Others may have sinned, and the inheritance of the sin is yours. Others may have sorely wronged you, and the hurt yet stays in your life. You never can be the same in this world that you might have been but for the wounding. You are not responsible for these marrings of your character which were wrought by others' hands. Still you are the builder, — you and God.

> "We are builders, and each one
> Should cut and carve as best he can;
> Every life is but a stone,
> Every one shall hew his own,
> Make or mar, shall every man."

Even the broken fragments of what seems a ruin you can take, and with them, through God's grace, you can make a noble fabric. It is strange how many of earth's most beautiful lives have grown up out of what seemed defeat and failure. Indeed, God seems to love to build spiritual loveliness out of the castaway fragments of lives, even out of sin's debris. In a great cathedral there is said to be a window, made by an apprentice out of the bits of stained glass that were thrown away as refuse and worthless waste when the other windows were made, and this is the most beautiful window of all. You can build a noble character for yourself, in spite of all the hurts and injuries done to you, wittingly or unwittingly, by others, with the fragments of the broken hopes and joys and the lost opportunities that lie strewn about your feet. No others by their worst work of hurt of marring can prevent your building a beautiful character for yourself.

When the ancient temple of Solomon was reared, the whole world was sought through, and its most costly and beautiful things were gathered and put into the sacred house. We should search everywhere for whatsoever things are true, whatsoever things are lovely, whatsoever things are pure, to build into our life. All that we can learn from books, from music, from art, from friends; all

that we can gather from the Bible and receive from the hand of
Christ himself, we should take and build into our character to
make it worthy. But in order to discover the things that are lovely
we must have the loveliness in our own soul. "Though we travel
the world over to find the beautiful," says one, "we must carry it
in our own heart, or, go where we may, we shall find it not." Only
a pure, true, loving heart can discover the things that are true,
pure, and loving to build in the character. We must have Christ in
us, and then we shall find Christly things everywhere, and gather
them into our own life.

There are some people who, in the discouragement of defeat and
failure, feel that it is then too late for them to make their character beautiful. They have lost their last opportunity, it seems to
them. But this is never true in the world in which Christ died. A
poet tells of walking in his garden and seeing a birds' nest lying
on the ground. The storm had swept through the tree and ruined
the nest. While he mused sadly over the wreck of the birds' home,
he looked up, and there he saw them building a new one amid
the branches. The birds teach us immortals a lesson. Though all
seems lost, let us not sit down and weep in despair, but let us
arise and begin to build again. No one can undo a wrong past. No
one can repair the ruins of years that are gone. We cannot live
our life over again. But, at our Father's feet, we can begin anew as
little children, and make all our life new.

> "Oh, to go back across the years long vanished,
> To have the words unsaid, the deeds undone,
> The errors cancelled, the deep shadows banished,
> In the glad sense of a new world begun:
> To be a little child, whose page of story
> Is yet undimmed, unblotted by a stain,
> And in the sunrise of primeval glory
> To know that life has had its start again!
> I may go back across the years long vanished;
> I may resume my childhood, Lord, in thee,
> When in the shadow of thy cross are banished
> All other shadows that encompass me;
> And o'er the road that now is dark and dreary,
> This soul, made buoyant by the strength of rest,
> Shall walk untired, shall run and not be weary,
> To bear the blessing that has made it blest."

Chapter 2

Our Undiscovered Faults

"A friend who holds a mirror to my face,
And, hiding none, is not afraid to face
My faults, my smallest blemishes, within;
Who friendly warns, reproves me if I sin—
Although it seems not so, he is my friend.

"But he who, ever flattering, gives me praise,
Who ne'er rebukes nor censures, nor delays
To come with eagerness and grasp my hand,
And pardon me, ere pardon I demand—
He is my enemy, although he seem my friend."

We may as well confess that it is not pleasant to be told of our faults. Poets and other writers tell us that he is our truest friend who does not shrink from holding the mirror to our face. Nevertheless, we do not like it. As a rule, he who proves such a friend to another finds himself a sinecure in his friendship thereafter. Even that may not be too great a price to pay, however, for the privilege of doing for one we love a service which shall take from his life a sad blemish or a serious flaw.

No doubt there are faults in us which we ourselves do not see. Our eyes are so set in our heads that they look out and not in. It is easier, therefore, for us to detect spots in others than in ourselves. So it comes that in most of us there are blemishes of which we are altogether unaware. The Bible speaks of sins of ignorance. So there are sins which we commit of which we are not conscious. In one of the Psalms there is a prayer to be cleansed, or cleared from, secret or hidden faults. So we have faults which are not seen by ourselves.

Then we all have in us many things, both good and bad, which our fellow-men cannot see, but of which we ourselves are aware. We cannot reveal ourselves perfectly, even to our own bosom companions. With no intention to hide anything, even desiring to live a perfectly open life, there will yet be many things in the inner depths of our being which our nearest friends cannot discover. No one but ourselves knows the motives that actuate us. Sometimes neighbors praise our good deed when we know well that the good was blurred by a self-seeking intent. Or others may criticize something we do, charging us with a wrong spirit, when we know in our heart that it was true love that prompted it.

We are both better and worse than others think us to be. The best things in good lives do not flash their beauty before human eyes. None of us can ever show to others all in us that is worthy. There are countless stars in the depths of the sky which no human eye ever sees. Human lives are deeper than the heavens in which the stars are set; and in the depths even of the most commonplace soul there are more splendors unrevealed to human gaze than are revealed. Who is there that says all the truth he tries to say, when he attempts to speak of or for his Master? What singer ever gets into his song all the music that is in his soul when he sings? What painter ever transfers to his canvas all the loveliness of the vision which fills his heart? What Christian ever lives out all the loyalty to Christ, all the purity and holiness, all the gentleness and sweetness, all the unselfishness and helpfulness, all the grace and beauty, he longs to show in his life? Even in those who fail and fall in defeat, and whose lives are little but shame and sin, there are yet gleams of beauty, like the shattered fragments of a once very noble ideal. We do not know what strivings, what penitences, what efforts to do better, what tears of sorrow, what hungerings after God and heaven, there are in the heart even of the depraved, in whom the world, even nearest friends, see nothing beautiful. No doubt in every life there is good which human eyes cannot see.

But there is evil, also, which our friends cannot detect, — things no one suspects, but of which we ourselves are painfully aware. Many a man goes out in the morning to be loved and welcomed by his friends, and praised and honored by the world, yet carrying in his own breast the memory of some deed of sin or shame committed in secret the night before. "If people only knew me," he says, "as I know myself to-day, they would scorn me instead of trusting me and honoring me." All of us are conscious of miserable things hidden within us, — secret habits wrought into fixed life, the play of unholy thoughts and feelings, the rising up of ugly passions and tempers, the movements of prides, vanity, self conceit, envy, jealousy, doubt, which do not reveal themselves to any eye without. There are evils in every one of which the person himself knows, but which others do not even suspect.

> "For no men or women that live to-day,
> Be they as good or as bad as they may,
> Even would dare to leave
> In faintest pencil or boldest ink
> All that they said or what they have done,
> What they have lived, and what they have felt,
> Under the stars or under the sun."

But there also are faults, unlovely things and sins in our hearts, of which we ourselves are unaware. There is an eye that pierces deeper than our own into our souls. In one place St. Paul says, "I know nothing against myself: yet am I not hereby justified; but he that judgeth me is the Lord." It is not enough to be innocent of conscious transgression; there are sins of ignorance. Only God sees us through and through. We must live for his inspection and approval.

We cannot see our own faults even as our neighbors see them. The Pharisee in his prayer, which really was not a prayer at all, spoke much of other people's sins, but saw none in himself. We are all much like him. We are prejudiced in our own favor. We are very charitable and tolerant toward our own shortcomings. We make all manner of allowance for our own faults, and are wonderfully patient with our own infirmities. We see our good things magnified, and our blemishes in a light that makes them seem almost virtues. So true is this, that if we were to meet ourself some day on the street, the self God sees, even the self our neighbor sees, we probably should not recognize it as really ourself. Our own judgment of our life is not conclusive. There is a self we do not see.

Then we cannot see into the future, to know whither the subtle tendencies of our life are leading us. We do many things which to our eyes appear innocent and harmless, but which have in them a hidden evil we cannot see. We indulge ourselves in many things which to us do not appear sinful, but which leave on our soul a touch of blight, a soiling of purity, of which we do not dream. We permit ourselves many little habits in which we see no danger, but which are silently entwining their invisible threads into a cable, which some day shall bind us hand and foot. We permit ourselves self-denials and sacrifices, thinking there is no reason why we should make them, unaware that we are lowering our standard of living, and permitting the subtle beginnings of self-indulgence to creep into our heart.

There is another class of hidden faults. Sin is deceitful. No doubt there are many things in most of us,— ways of living, traits of character, qualities of disposition, — which we consider, perhaps, among our strong points, or at least fair and commendable things in us, which in God's eye are not only flaws and blemishes, but sins. Good and evil in certain qualities do not lie very far apart. It is quite easy for devotion to principle to shade off into obstinacy. It is easy for self-respect, consciousness of ability, to pass over into miserable anger, when the truth is, he is only giving way to very bad temper. It is easy to let gentleness become weakness, and tolerance toward sinners tolerance toward sin. It is easy for us to become very selfish in many phases of our conduct, while in general we are really quite unselfish. For example: A man may be giving his life to the good of his fellows in the larger sense, while in his own home he is utterly regardless of the comfort and convenience of those nearest to him. Without, he is polite, thoughtful, kindly; within, he cares not how much trouble he causes, exacting and demanding attention and service, and playing the petty tyrant instead of the large-hearted, generous Christian. Who of us does not have little or greater secret blemishes lying alongside his most shining virtues? We do not see them in ourselves. We see the faults cropping out in our neighbor, and we say, "What a pity so fine a character is so marred!" And our neighbor looks at us and says, "What a pity that with so much that is good, he has so many marring faults!" Sin is deceitful.

The substance of all that has been said is, that besides the faults our neighbors see in us, besides those our closest friends see, besides those of which we ourselves are aware, all of us have undiscovered errors in our life, hidden, secret faults, of which only God knows.

If we are living truly, we want to find every flaw or blemish there is in us, of whatever kind. He is a coward who shrinks from the discovery of his own faults. We should be glad always to learn of any hidden unloveliness in ourselves. Some one says, "Count yourself richer that day you discover a new fault in yourself — not richer because it is there, but richer because it is no longer a hidden fault; and if you have not yet found all your faults, pray to have them revealed to you, even if the revelation must come in a way that hurts your pride."

It is dangerous to allow any faults, however small, to stay in our life; but hidden faults are even more perilous than those of which we are aware. They are enemies concealed, traitors in the camp, unrecognized, passing for friends. No good, true, and brave man will allow a discovered sin of fault to stay unchallenged in his life; but an undiscovered sin lurks and nests in a man's heart, and breeds its deadly evil in his very soul. Before he is aware of its presence, it may eat out the heart of his manhood, and poison the very springs of his being.

Hidden faults, remaining undiscovered and uncured in us, will hinder our spiritual growth, and we shall not know the reason for our moral weakness, or lack of power. They will also defeat the working out of the divine plan in our life. When Canove, the great sculptor, was about to begin work upon his statue of Napoleon, it is said that his keen eye saw a tiny red line running through the upper part of the splendid block of marble out of which he was to carve the statue. The stone had been brought at great expense from Paros for this express purpose. Common eyes saw no flaw in it, but the sculptor saw it, and would not use the marble.

May it not be so ofttimes with lives which face great opportunities? God's eye sees in them some undiscovered flaw or fault, some tiny line of marring color. God desires truth in the inward parts. The life that pleases him must be pure and white throughout. He who clings to faults discovered, refusing to cast them out, or he who refuses to let the candle of the Lord search out the hidden faults in him, that he may put them away, is marring his own destiny. God cannot use him for the larger, nobler task or trust for which he had planned to use him. The tiny red line running through the marble causes it to be set aside and rejected. What shall we do? God alone can know our hidden faults. We must ask him to search our hearts and try our ways, and to cleanse our lives of whatsoever evil thing he finds in us. Our prayer should be,—

'Who can discern his errors?
Clear thou me from hidden faults."

Chapter 3

Life's second chance

"Winter makes ready for the spring
By months of struggle and suffering;
And the victory won from the mortal strife
Strengthens the fibre and pulse of life.
How if the earth in its chill despair
Felt that the fight were too hard to bear,
Where were the bloom and the vintage then?
Where were the harvest for hungering men?"
~Susan Coolidge.

If we had but one chance in life it would fare badly with most of us. We do scarcely anything perfectly the first time we try to do it. Nearly always do we fail. Not many lives are lived beautifully, without a break or a lapse, from childhood to age. If, therefore, the opportunity of choosing good came to us only once, and was then forever withdrawn, few of us would make anything of our life. We are in the habit of saying that opportunities never come twice to us One writes,—

"Never comes the chance that passed:
That one moment was its last.
Though thy life upon it hung,
Though thy death beneath it swung,
If thy future all the way
Now in darkness goes astray,
When the instant born of fate
Passes through the golden gate,
When the hour, but not the man,
Comes and goes from Nature's plan—
Nevermore that time shall be
Burden-bearer into thee.
Weep and search o'er land and main,
Lost chance never comes again."

This is all true, but it is not the whole truth. No single opportunity comes twice, but other opportunities come. Though we have failed once, that is not the end. The past is irrevocable; but while there is even the smallest margin of life remaining, there is yet another chance.

Jeremiah tells us of visiting a potter's house, and watching the potter as he wrought on the wheels. His work was marred in his hands in some way. But instead of throwing it away, he made it into another vessel. The second vessel was not so beautiful as the one the potter first intended to make, but it was useful. The clay had a second chance.

The prophet's parable had its first meaning for his own people, but its lesson is for all time. For one thing, it tells us that God has a plan for every life. The potter has a pattern after which he intends to fashion his vessel. For every human life there is a divine pattern, something which God means it to become. This first thought of God for our lives is the very best thing possible for them.

We learn, again, from this ancient acted parable that our lives may be marred in the living, so that they shall never attain God's beautiful thought for them. There is a difference, however, between a lump of clay and a human life. The marring of the clay may be the potter's fault, or it may be the result of an accident; at least, it cannot be the fault of the clay itself. If a misshapen jar or bowl comes into your hands, you would not say, "what a careless piece of clay it was that made itself into this irregular form!" Rather you would say, "What a careless potter it was that spoiled this vessel, when he had the soft clay in his hands!" But when a life is marred, and fails of the beauty and nobleness which it was designed to have, you can not blame God. You cannot say, "I was clay on the wheel, and the great Potter gave the wrong touch, and spoiled the loveliness that ought to have been wrought in my life." You are not clay, but a human soul. You have a will, and God does not shape you as the potter moulds his plastic clay. He works through your own will, and you can resist him, and can defeat his purpose for your life, and spoil the noble design into which he would fashion you. The blotches in this fair world are all the sad work of human hands, never of God's hands.

But this is not all of the lesson. The potter took the clay again when the vessel he meant to make was marred, and with it made another vessel. The second could not be so fine nor so large as the first would have been but for the marring. Yet it was better that there should be an inferior vessel made than that the clay should be thrown away. It is thus that God deals with human souls. He does not cast off the life that has failed of its first and best possibilities. Even in the ruins of a soul there are divine elements, and so long as a little fragment remains God wants to give it still another chance.

It is said that one day Carlyle suddenly stopped at a street crossing, and, stooping down, picked up something out of the mud, even at the risk of being knocked down and run over by passing vehicles. With his bare hands he gently rubbed the mud off this thing which he had picked up, holding it as carefully and touching it as gently as if it had be something of great value. He took it to the pavement and laid it down on a clean spot on the curbstone. "That," said the old man, in a tone of sweetness he rarely used, "is only a crust of bread. Yet I was taught by my mother never to waste anything, and, above all, bread, more precious than gold. I am sure that the little sparrows, or a hungry dog, will get nourishment form this bit of bread."

This is a suggestion of the way God looks upon a human life which bears his image. The merest fragment of life he regards as sacred. So long as there is the least trace of divine possibility in a human soul, he is ready to make something out of it, to take it out of the mire and give it another chance. "The vessel that he made was marred in the hands of the potter; so he made it again, — another vessel."

In Florence, one of the treasures of art admired by thousands of visitors is Michael Angelo's representation in marble of the young David. The shepherd boy stands with firm foothold, the stone grasped tightly in his right hand, ready to be sped on its holy errand. When the statue was inveiled, three hundred and fifty years ago, it caused an unparalleled sensation among all lovers of art. It is, indeed, a marvelous piece of sculpture.

But the strangely winning thing is the story of that statue is, that it was the stone's second chance. A sculptor began work on a noble piece of marble, but, lacking skill he only hacked and marred the block. It was then abandoned as spoiled and worthless, and cast aside. For years it lay in a back yard, soiled and blackened, half hidden among the rubbish. At last Angelo saw it, and at once perceived its possibilities. Under his skillful hand the stone was cut into the fair and marvelous beauty which appears in the statue of David. Yet it is said that the completed work is not quite perfect; that because of the first cutting of the stone the final result is marred.

This is another form of the parable of the potter. From a spoiled and castaway block was hewn this splendid work of art. Though a life has been spoiled by unskillful hands, so that it seems as if all were lost, there is one, the great Sculptor, who can take the marred, disfigured block, now lying soiled amid the world's rubbish, and from it carve yet a marvel of beauty, — if not all that it might once have been, at least a very beautiful character.

There is a little poem that tells of a bird with a broken wing which one found in a woodland meadow: —

> "I healed it's wound, and each morning
> It sang its old sweet strain;
> But the bird with the broken pinion
> Never soared as high again.
>
> I found a young life broken
> By sin's seductive art;
> And, touched with a childlike pity,
> I took him to my heart.
>
> He lived with a noble purpose,
> And struggled not in vain;
> But the life that sin had stricken
> Never soared as high again.
>
> Yet the bird with the broken pinion
> Kept another from the snare;
> And the life that sin had stricken
> Raised another from despair."

This little poem teaches two lessons. One is, that the second chance is not so good as the first. The bird with the broken wing never soared as high again as it had soared before. The young life which sin had broken, but which grace had headed, never was quite so beautiful again as before it was stricken, never soared so high in its flight as it would have done if sin had not hurt it.

There is an impression among some people that a man is a better man after having tasted sin, after knowing evil by experience, then repenting, being forgiven, and restored. This is a mistaken impression. Innocence is far better than despair; but a life is never so beautiful after sin's fires have swept over it as it would have been if it had been kept untarnished, and had realized God's first thought for it. The bird with the broken pinion never soared so high again. There are some things we never get over. The wounds may be healed, but the scars remain. There are some losses we can never get back. Esau wept bitterly over the losing of his birthright, but wept in vain; he never could get again what he had profanely bartered off for a trifle. Lost innocence never can be restored.

The other lesson which the poem teaches is the same we have found already in the parable of the potter. The bird with the broken pinion was not useless; it kept another bird form the snare. Through its own hurt it had gotten a power of helpfulness which it never could have had without its experience of wounding and marring. The same is true of human lives which have failed and have fallen into sin.

> "The life that sin had stricken,
> Raised another form despair."

There is not doubt that there is a work possible to those who have been hurt in sin's battle and have been lifted up again which they never could have done without the sad experience through which they have passed. John B. Gough never could have pleaded with such burning eloquence for temperance, as he did for so many years, of he had never himself known from experience the terrible bitterness of the curse of strong drink. His own life was marred by the dissipation which marked his earlier years, and which dragged him down into debasement; and he could never win the nobleness and beauty which would have been possible to him if he had never so failed and sinned against himself. But he took his second chance when the first was lost forever, and grew into great strength of character and into abounding usefulness. It is even doubtful if he would ever have made so much of his life, had it not been for the losing of its first chance, and the imperiling of all, which wrought afterward in him as such mighty motives, impelling him to such heroic life and such noble service for his fellow-men.

The lesson is plain. It is for all of us. It is not for one great experience alone, but has its perpetual application; for we are continually missing the things which are the first and the very best in life's opportunities. It is sad that we do this, and we should rigidly train ourselves to make the most we can of every chance in life that comes to us. But when we have failed, we should not spend a moment in regret; for regret is vain and useless, and only helps to eat away the strength that remains. We should turn instantly and with resistless energy to the saving of what is left. There is always another chance, even down to the life's latest moment in this world.

Chapter 4

Getting Help from Criticism

"So, take and use thy work,
Amend what flaws may lurk,
What strain o' the stuff, what warpings past the aim!
My times be in thy hand!
Perfect the cup as planned!
Let age approve of youth, and death complete the same."
~Robert Browning.

PERFECTION in life and character should be the aim of every life. Our prayer should ever be to be fashioned into spotless beauty. No matter what the cost may be, we should never shrink from any thing that will teach us a new lesson, or put a new touch of loveliness into our character.

We get our lessons from many teachers. We read in books fair lines which set holy tasks of attainment for us. We see in other lives lovely things which inspire in us noble longings. We learn by experience, and we grow by exercise. We may get many a lesson, too, from those among whom we live. People ought to be a means of grace to us. Mere contact of life with life is refining and stimulating.

"Iron sharpeneth iron:
So a man sharpeneth the countenance of his friend."

The world is not always friendly to us. It is not disposed always to pat us on the back, or to pet and praise us. One of the first things a young man learns, when he pushes out from his own home, where everybody dotes on him, is that he must submit to criticism and opposition. Not all he does receives commendation. But this very condition is healthful. Our growth is much more wholesome in such an atmosphere, than where we have only adulation and praise.

We ought to get profit from criticism. Two pairs of eyes should see more than one. None of us have all the wisdom there is in the world. However wise any of us may be, there are others who know some things better than we know them, and who can make valuable and helpful suggestions to us, at least concerning some points of our work. The shoemaker never could have painted the picture, but he could criticize the buckle when he stood before the canvas which the great artist had covered with his noble creations; and the artist was wise enough to welcome the criticism and quickly amend his picture, to make it correct. Of course the shoemaker knows more about shoes, and the tailor or the dressmaker more about clothes, and the furniture-maker more about furniture, than the artist does. The criticisms of these artisans on the things in their own special lines ought to be of great value to the artist, and he would be a very foolish painter who would sneer at their suggestions and refuse to profit by them.

The same is true in other things besides art. No one's knowledge is really universal. None of us know more than a few fragments of the great mass of knowledge. There are some things somebody else knows better than you do, however wide your range of intelligence may be. There are very humble people who could give you suggestions well worth taking on certain matters concerning which they have more correct knowledge than you have. If you wish to make your work perfect you most condescend to take hints and information from any one and every one who may be ready to give it to you.

It is true, also, that others can see faults and imperfections in us which we ourselves cannot see. We are too closely identified with our own life and work to be unprejudiced observers or just critics. We can never make the most and the best of our life if we refuse to be taught by other than ourselves. A really self-made man is very poorly made, because he is the product of only one man's thought. The strong things in his own individuality are likely to be emphasized to such a degree that they become idiosyncrasies, while on other sides his character is left defective. The best-made man is the one who in his formative years has the benefit of wholesome criticism. His life is developed on all sides. Faults are corrected. His nature is restrained at the points where the tendency is to overgrowth, while points of weakness are strengthened. We all need, not only as a part of our education, but in all our life and work, the corrective influence of the opinions and suggestions of other.

"Oh wad some power the giftie gie us

To see oursel's as ithers see us!
It wad frae mony a blunder free us
And foolish notion."

But in order to get profit from criticism, we must relate ourselves to it in a sympathetic and receptive way. We must be ready
to hear and give hospitable thought to the things that others may
say of us and of what we are doing. Some people are only hurt,
never helped, by criticism, even when it is most sincere. They regard it always as unkindly, and meet it with a bitter feeling. They
resent it, from whatever source it may come, and in whatever
form, as something impertinent. They regard it as unfriendly, as
a personal assault against which they must defend themselves.
They seem to think of their own life as something fenced about
by such sanctities, that no other person can with propriety offer
even a suggestion concerning anything that is theirs, unless it
be in the way of commendation. They have such opinions of the
infallibility of their own judgment, and the flawless excellence of
their own performance, that it seems never to occur to them as a
possibility that the judgment of others might add further wisdom,
or point out anything better. So they utterly refuse to accept criticism, however kindly, or any suggestion which looks to anything
different from what they have done.

We all know people of this kind. So long as others will compli-
ment them on their work, they give respectful attention and are
pleased; but the moment a criticism is made, however slight, or
even the question whether something else would not be an improvement is asked, they are offended. They regard as an enemy
any one who even intimates disapproval of who hints, however
delicately, that this or that might be otherwise.

It is hard to maintain cordial relations of friendship with such
persons, for no one cares to be forbidden to express an opinion
that is not an echo of another's. Not many people will take the
touble to keep a lock on the door if their lips all the while for fear of
offending a self-conceited friend. Then one who rejects and resents
all criticism cuts himself off from one of the best means of growth
and improvement. He is no longer teachable, and, therefore, is no
longer a learner. He would rather keep his faults than be humbled
by being told of them in order to have them corrected. So he pays
no heed to what any person has to say about his work, and gets
no benefit whatever from the opinions and judgments of others.

Such a spirit is very unwise. Infinitely better is it that we keep ourselves always ready to receive instruction from every source. We are not making the most of our life if we are not eager to do our best in whatever we do, and to make constant progress in our doing. In order to do this, we must continually be made aware of the imperfections of our performances that we may correct them. No doubt it hurts our pride to be told of our faults, but we would better let the pain work amendment than work resentment. Really, we ought to be thankful to any one who shows us a blemish in our life, which we then can have removed. No friend is truer and kinder to us than be who does this, for he helps us to grow into nobler and more beautiful character.

Of course there are different ways of pointing out a fault. One person does it bluntly and harshly, almost rudely. Another will find a way to make us aware of our faults without causing us any felling of humiliation. Doubtless it is more pleasant to have our correction come in this gentle way. It is also the more Christian way to give it. Great wisdom is required in those who would point out faults in others. They need deep love in their own heart that they may truly seek the good of those in whom they detect the flaws or errors, and not criticize in a spirit of exultation. Too many take delight in discovering faults in other people and in pointing them out. Others do it only when they are in anger, blurting out their sharp criticisms in fits of bad temper. We should all seek to possess the spirit of Christ, who was most patient and gentle in telling his friends wherein they failed.

Harm is done ofttimes by the want of this spirit in those whose duty it is to teach others. St. Paul enjoins fathers not to provoke their children to wrath, lest they be discouraged. There are parents who almost never correct their children to save anger. They are continually telling them of their faults, as if their whole existence were a dreary and impertinent mistake, and as if parents can fulfil their duty to their children only by continually nagging at them and scolding them.

Those who are anointed to train and teach the young have a tremendous responsibility for the wise and loving exercise of the power that is theirs. We should never criticize or correct, save in love. If we find ourselves in anger or cherishing any bitter, unkind, or resentful feeling, as we are about to point out an error or a mistake in another person, or in the other's work, we would better be silent and not speak until we can speak in love. Only when our heart is full of love are we fit to judge another, or to tell him of his faults.

But while this is the Christian way for all who would make criticisms of others, it is true also, that however we learn of our faults, however ungentle and unsympathetic the person may be who makes us aware of them, we would better accept the correction in a humble, loving way and profit by it. Perhaps few of us hear the honest truth about ourselves until some one grows angry with us and blurts it out in bitter words. It may be an enemy who says the severe thing about us, or it may be some one who is base and unworthy of respect; but whoever it may be, we would better ask whether there may not be some truth in the criticism, and if there be, then set ourselves to get clear of it. In whatever way we are made aware of a fault we ought to be grateful for the fact; for the discovery gives us an opportunity to rise to a better, nobler life, or to a higher and finer achievement.

There are people whose criticisms are not such as can profit us. It is easy to find fault even with the noblest work. Then there are those who are instinctive fault-finders, regarding it as their privilege, almost their duty, to give an opinion on every subject that comes before them, and to offer some criticism on every piece of work that they see. Their opinions, however, are usually valueless, and ofttimes it requires much patience to receive them graciously, without showing irritation. But even in such cases, when compelled to listen to loquacious animadversions from those who know nothing what ever of the matters concerning which they speak so authoritatively, we would do well to receive all criticisms and suggestions in good temper and without impatience.

An interesting story of Michael Angelo is related, which illustrates the wise way of treating even ignorant, officious, and impertinent criticism. When the artist's great statue of David was place for the first time in the Plaza in Florence, all the people were hushed in wonder before its noble majesty — all except Soderinni. This man looked at the statue from different points of view with a wise, critical air, and then suggested that the nose was a little too long. The great sculptor listened quietly to the suggestion, and taking his chisel and mallet, he set a ladder against the stature, in order to reach the face, and climbed up, carrying a little marble dust in his hand. Then he seemed to be working carefully upon the objectionable feature, as if changing it to suit his critic's taste, letting the marble dust fall as he wrought. When he came down Soderinni again looked at the figure, now from this point of view and then from that, at last expressing entire approval. His suggestion had been accepted, as he supposed, and he was satisfied.

The story furnishes a good illustration of a great deal of fault-finding to which we must listen. It is unintelligent and valueless. But it cannot be restrained. There is not subject under heaven on which these wise people do not claim to have a right to express an opinion, and there is no work so perfect that they cannot point out where it is faulty and might be improved. They are awed by no greatness. Such criticisms are worthy only of contempt, and such critics do not deserve courteous attention. But it is better that we treat them with patience. It helps at least in our own selfdiscipline, and it is the nobler way.

This, then, is the lesson — that we should not resent criticism whether it be made in a kindly or in an unkindly way; that we should be eager and willing to learn form any one, since even the humblest and most ignorant man knows something better than we do and is able to be our teacher at some point; that the truth always should be welcomed — especially the truth about ourselves, that which affects our own life and work,— however it may wound our pride and humble us, or however its manner of coming to us may hurt us; and that the moment we learn of anything that is not beautiful in us, we should seek its correction. Thus only can we ever reach the best things in character or in achievement.

Chapter 5

Fellow-workers with God

"Who doeth good by loving deed or word;
Who lifteth up a fallen one or dries a tear;
Who helps another bear his heavy cross,
Or on the parched and fevered lips doeth pour
A blessed draught of water sweet and cool.
Becomes co-worker with the Lord of all."

There are many things which God does, in which we can have no part. A child wished he could be a painter, that he might help God paint the clouds and skies and sunsets. God wants no help in this work. He wrought unhelped by creature-hand in making the worlds. In providence, too, he has no fellow-worker. No one assists him in keeping the stars in their orbits, in sending rains and dews and summer sunshine. No one helps him paint the roses and the lilies.

But there are other things in which God permits us to be his co-workers. He calls us up close beside him to work with him, doing a part while he does a part. A story is told of an artist who greatly desired to have a share in the decorating of a famous building. If he could not do it all, he asked that he might be permitted to paint one panel of one of the great doors. If this request could not be granted, he craved to be allowed at least to hold the brushes for the master who should do the work. If it was deemed to be such an honor and privilege to do even the smallest part on a building of only earthly glory, what an honor it is to work with Christ in the building of his great spiritual temple!

Yet this privilege is ours. We may not help God paint his clouds and sunsets, but we can put tints of immortal beauty upon human souls. In a certain sense we are fellow-workers with God in all the affairs of our lives. We often imagine we are doing certain fine things without God's help. But we are not. A man makes great inventions, constructs wonderful machines, harnesses steam and electricity, and says, "See what I have done!" But who puts into nature the mysterious forces and energies which he has made available for practical use? In their inventions and discoveries, men only find the powers God stored away ages since. Men are only discoverers and adjusters. They run wires on poles, or lay cables in the sea; but the currents that flash through them carrying messages of business, commerce, joy, sorrow, come from God's hidden reserves of energy. Men are working with God, and their part is small.

In spiritual life it is also true that we are fellow-workers with God. He calls us to stand beside him and do a part while he does a part. When a mother, with great joy in her heart, takes her baby into her arms and looks into it face, God says to her, "Take this child, and nurse it for me." It is God's child. He wants it trained, its powers developed, so that when at length the man stands before his tasks he may not fail, but may do them well. Yet God gives into the mother's hand the duty of nursing the child for him, teaching it, putting into its heart gentle thoughts, wooing out the sweet love that sleeps there, and thus preparing the life for its place and work. Yet alone she cannot do anything. God and the mother are fellow-workers in the training of the life.

The teacher sits down with his class. The end of the teaching is, the bringing of the scholars to Christ, the building up in them of a Christian character, and the leading of them out into ways of usefulness and loving service. What is the teacher's part? He can make plain to his class the word and will of God, and he can also represent Christ to them, showing them in his own life glimpses of the diving compassion, tenderness, yearning, truth, purity, and love. But he cannot himself do what needs to be done in their young lives; only God can do that. But God works through the teacher. God and he are fellow-workers.

So it is in all Christian work. We have our part. God has ordained that the heavenly treasure shall be put in earthen vessels. We must never forget, however, that we are not doing the work ourselves. Saddest of all things in Christian workers is the losing out of the heart of the sense of dependence upon God, the leaving out of Christ, the feeling that they are doing the things alone. God will work through us only when we humbly, in faith and love and self-renunciation, lay ourselves into his hands, that his life may flow through us into the lives we are seeking to bless.

We are the chisel with which God carves his statues. Unquestionably we must do the work. Our hands must touch men's lives and beautify them. The mother, the teacher, the Christian friend, must carve and mould the life of the child into the beauty of the Lord. But the human worker is only the chisel. The sculptor needs his chisel, but the chisel can do nothing, produce no beauty, of itself. We must put ourselves into Christ's hand that he may use us.

There is a hallowing influence in this thought that we are working beside God in what he is doing on immortal lives. Are we worthy to do it? Hawthorne, speaking of a block of marble and the possibilities of beauty that lie in it, waiting to be brought out, said that the stone assumed a sacred character, and that no man should dare touch it unless he felt within himself a consecration and priesthood. If this be true when it is only a block of marble that is to be wrought upon, how much more is it true of a human soul, — a child's life, for example, laid in a mother's arms; any life laid in your hands or mine, — we may free the angel that waits within it! It is a most sacred moment when a life is put before us to be touched by us.

Suppose that the mother, — suppose that you or I, — should not do the holy work well, and the life should be marred, hurt, stunted, its beauty blurred, its purity stained, its development impaired, its power weakened; think of the sadness of the result. How sweet the mother must keep her own spirit, how gentle, how patient, how pure and true, while she is working with God in nursing her child for him! How heavenly must the teacher keep his temper, how quiet, how unselfish, how Christlike, when he is sitting beside the Master, working with him on the lives of the scholars! How softly we should all walk continually, with reverent, chastened, uplifted feeling and hallowed spirit, as we remember that we are fellow-workers with God!

There is here also a strong impulse to faithfulness. The work we do for God and with God we must do well. We are tempted to say, "My part is not important; it is so small. It cannot matter much to God whether I do it well or ill. He does not need my little part." But that is not true. Our least part is important. God needs our faithfulness. He needs the mother in training the child, — needs the most conscientious, most painstaking, most beautiful work she can do. If her hand slacks even only for one day, doing its part carelessly, less than faithfully, there may be a blemish, a marring in the child's life, which shall reveal itself years hence. The completeness of the finished work depends always on our doing our best. We rob God if we are ever less than faithful.

There is special encouragement in this truth for those who feel unequal to the duty that the Master assigns to them. They see others who do beautiful things that bless and brighten the world, but it seems to them that all they can do is so commonplace, so homely, so full of blurring and fault, that it is not worth while for them to do it at all. But the clumsiest hands truly surrendered to God may do work that is most beautiful in his sight.

Long ago, in quaint old Nuremberg, lived two boys, Albrecht Dürer and Franz Knigstein. Both wished to be artists, and both studied and wrought with great earnestness. Albrecht had genius; but Franz had only love for art, without the power to put on canvas the beautiful visions that haunted him. Years passed, and they planned to make each an etching of the Lord's Passion. When the compared their work, that of Franz was cold and lifeless, while Albrecht's was instinct with beauty and pathos. Then Franz saw it all, and knew that he could never be an artist. His heart was almost broken; but he said in a voice choked with tears, yet full of manly courage, "Franz, the good Lord gave me no such give as this of yours; but something, some homely duty, he has waiting somewhere for me to do. Yet now — be you artist of Nuremberg, and I"—

"Stay, Franz be still one moment," cried Albrecht, seizing his pencil. Franz supposed Albrecht was adding some finishing touches to his exquisite drawing, and waited patiently in his attitude of surrender, his hands folding together. With his swift pencil Albrecht drew a few lines and showed the sketch to his friend.

"Why, those are only my hands," said Franz. "Why did you take them?" — "I took them" said Albrecht, "as you stood there making the sad surrender of your life so very bravely. I said to myself, 'Those hands that may never paint a picture can now most certainly make one.' I have faith in those folded hands, my brother-friend. They will go into men's hearts in the days to come."

Albrecht's words were true prophecy. Into the world of love and duty has gone the story so touching and helpful in its beautiful simplicity; and into the world of art has gone the picture — for Albrecht Dürer's famous "Folded Hands" is but a picture of the hands of Franz Knigstein as they were folded that day in sweet, brave resignation, when he gave up his heart's dearest wish, and yet believed that the Lord had some homely duty still worth his doing.

This charming story tells us that if we cannot do the beautiful things we see others doing for Christ and which we long to do, we can at least do some lowly work for him. It teaches us, too, that self-surrender to God, though our heart's fondest hope is laid down, is, in God's sight, really the most beautiful thing we can do with our life. It teaches us also, that the hands which can do no brilliant thing for God, may yet become hands of benediction in the world. If we are truly fellow-workers with God, he can use whatever we have that we really surrender to him. And ofttimes he can do more with our failures than with our successes.

Then not only are we fellow-workers with God, but also with each other. Sometimes we are tempted to be envious of others who are working by our side. They seem to overshadow us. It hurts us to hear them praised. It appears to us as if they wronged us in some way, by drawing off some measure of attention from us, by obscuring our little work in the brilliance of their larger or more conspicuous achievement. It should cure us of all such miserable feelings to remember that in God's perfect plan each has his own particular part to do in the great whole. The work of our brother next to us is his, not ours. We could not do it, even if he were not in his place. The fact that he does his part well, and receives approval and commendation, will not detract from our commendation if we are faithful in our own place.

The work of no one is more than a fragment at the best. Nobody finishes anything in this world. The strongest, the most skillful, the longest-lived, only puts a few touches on something of God's. Perhaps he begins a piece of new work, and then leaves it for others to continue; or perhaps he enters into the labor of others who have come before him, carrying it on a little farther. One sows, another reaps — we are co-workers. Our work well done will be all the more perfect if those who work with us do their part well; and no matter how others are praised, God's approval of us will depend upon our own faithfulness.

> "What matter, friend, though you and I
> May sow, and others gather?
> We build and other occupy.
> Each laboring for the other.
> What though we toil from sun to sun,
> And men forget to flatter?
> The noblest work our hands have done—
> If God approve, what matter?"

Chapter 6

Our Debt to Others

"Brother, we are surely bound
On the same journey, and our eyes alike
Turn up and onward; wherefore, now thou risest,
Lean on mine arm, and let us for a space
Pursue the path together."
~Buchanan

The true standard of greatness is service. It is not what our life is in gifts, in culture, in strength, but what we do with our life, that is the real test of character. Our Lord taught this truth when he said, "Whosoever would become great among you shall be your minister; and whoso ever would be first among you shall be you servant." It has been well said: "He only is great of heart who floods the world with a great affection. He only is great of mind who stirs the world with great thoughts. He only is great of will who does something to shape the world to a great career. And he is greatest who does the most of all these things and does them best." We are to hold all that is in us at the service of our fellow-men, in Christ's name.

St. Paul speaks of himself as debtor to every one, Greek and barbarian, wise and foolish. It was love that he owed, — the only kind of debt that he believed in. "Owe no man anything," he said elsewhere, "save to love one another." Love is a debt which never can be altogether settled. You may pay it all off to-day, but tomorrow you will find it heavy as ever. It is a debt which everybody owes to everybody. Nor can it be paid off with any mere sentimental love. It cost St. Paul a great deal to settle his obligations and pay his debts to other men. There is a sort of philanthropic sentiment which some people have which does not cost them very much, — an eloquent speech now and then in behalf of their pet cause, and perhaps an occasional contribution of money. But to pay his debts to men, St. Paul gave up all he had, and then gave himself up to service, suffering, and sacrifice to the very uttermost. Loving always costs. We cannot save our own life and pay the debts of love we owe.

We are in debt to everybody. It is not hard to recognize this indebtedness to the gentle, cultured, well-to-do Greeks. Anybody can love them and be kind to them, they are so beautiful and sweet. The trouble is with the barbarians. They are not of "our set;" they are not refined. They are rude and wicked; they are heathens. It is not so hard, either, to love them in a philanthropic way as heathens, far off and out of our sight, as it is in a close, personal, practical way, when they come to live next door to us, and when we must meet them every day. But the truth is, we are as really debtors to these barbarians as we are to the Greeks. Perhaps our debt to them is even greater, because they need us more.

It is well that we should get a very clear idea of our true relation as Christians to all other people. We owe Love to every one, and love always serves. Serving is an essential quality of love. Love does not stand among people commanding attention and demanding to be ministered unto, exacting rights, honor, respect. Love seeks to give, to minister, to be of use, to do good to others. There are many people who want to have friends, meaning by friends pleasant persons who will come into their comfort, who will advance their interests, who will flatter their vanity, who will make living easier for them. But that is not the way Christ would define friendship. He would put it just the other way. The true Christian desire is to be a friend to others, to do things for them, to minister to their comfort, to further their interests, to be a help and a blessing to them. That was St. Paul's thought when he said that he was a debtor to every man. He wanted to be every one's ministering friend. When a man stood before him, Paul's heart yearned to do him good in some way, went out to him in loving thought, longed to impart to him some spiritual gift, to add to his comfort, happiness, or usefulness. It is thus we should relate ourselves to every human being who comes within our influence. To every person we meet we have an errand. One has put it well in the following lines:

> "Every soul that touches yours—
> Be it the slightest contact—
> Gets therefrom some good;
> Some little grace; one kindly thought;
> One aspiration yet unfelt;
> One bit of courage
> For the darkening sky;

One gleam of faith
To brave the thickening ills of life;
One glimpse of brighter skies
Beyond the gathering mists—
To make this life worth while
And heaven a surer heritage."

This does not mean that we should be officious and obtrusive in pressing our help upon those we meet. There is a story of one whose prayer was that he might be permitted to do a great deal of good without even knowing it. That is the best helpfulness which flows out of the heart and life as light from a star, as fragrance from a flower. Love works most effectively when it works unconsciously, almost instinctively, inspired from within. Then it bestows its blessing or does its good unobtrusively. You friend does not come to you and say, "I want to cheer you up. I want to cure you of that bad habit. I want to give you more wisdom. I want to help you to be noble." If he came thus, announcing with flourish of trumpets his benevolent intention toward you, he would probably defeat his purpose. But he comes as your friend, with no programme, no heralding of his desire; comes loving you, and bringing into your life the best that is in his own life, sincerely yearning in some way to be a help to you. Then virtue passes from him to you, and new happiness and blessing come to you from him, you know not how. You have new courage, new gladness, new inspiration. Sin seems even more ignoble and unworthy, and holiness shines with brighter radiance. You are strengthened in your purpose to live worthily. You are more eager to make the most of your life. Thus love unconsciously, and without any definite plan, quickens and inspires another life to do its best. There is no other way of paying our debt to others which is so Christlike as this. Love gives itself, its own very life, to become life to others.

"O Lord! That I could waste my life for others,
With no ends of my own;
That I could pour myself into my brothers,
And live for them alone!"

The whole drift of Christian teaching and impulse is on the line of this lesson. Our Lord's definitions and illustrations of love all emphasize this quality of helpful serving. "Not to be ministered unto, but to minister," was the saying that epitomized the whole motive of his own blessed life. The good Samaritan was the Master's ideal of the working of love in human experience. When asked who was greatest in the kingdom of heaven, his reply was very plain and clear, — he who serves the most fully and the most unselfishly.

St. Paul, who so wondrously caught the spirit of his Master, has many words which show varying phases of the truth that love's very essential quality is unselfish helpfulness, the carrying of the life with all its rich gifts and powers in such a way that it may be a blessing to every other life it touches. "Love seeketh not its own." Its thought and service are for others. "Ye ought to help the weak." "We then that are strong ought to bear the infirmities of the weak, and not to please ourselves." There are those who are weak in body, and must lean on the strength of others. We ofttimes see illustrations of this in homes where the invalid of the household draws the strength of all the family to his helping. But physical weakness is not the only weakness. There are those who are spiritually weak, — feeble in purpose, broken by long sinning, until almost no strength remains in them, or enfeebled by sorrow. The law of love, that the strong should bear the infirmities of the weak, is quite as applicable in the sphere of life as in the case of physical weakness.

"Lift a little—lift a little!
Many they who need thine aid,
Many lying on the roadside
'Neath misfortune's dreary shade.

Pass not by, like priest and Levite,
Heedless of thy fellow-man;
But with heart and arms extended
Be the good Samaritan."

In these late days men are doing wonderful things for those who are suffering from infirmities. They educate the blind, until the privation of blindness is almost blotted out. They teach the dumb to speak. They take imbeciles and the feeble-minded, and with almost infinite patience they find the soul, as it were, that lies hidden in the remote depths of the being, and call it out, ofttimes restoring to sanity and to usefulness lives that seemed hopelessly imbecile. This is very beautiful. It is all the work of Christianity. Heathen civilization had no sympathy with weakness, and no patience with it. The sickly child, they said, would better die. The lame, the blind, the dumb, the insane, were simply cast out to perish. Christianity has filled the world with love. The other night four of the wisest physicians in a great city sat by a young child's crib through all the watches, doing all that science and skill could do to save the little one's life. It is Christianity that has taught such lessons as this.

We want the same interest in the spiritual helping of those who are weak. Those who are strong should give of their strength to support and uphold the weak. Those have experience should become guides to the inexperienced. Those who have been comforted should carry comfort to those who are sorrowing. We are to be to others what Jesus would be if he were in our place. The best that is in us should ever be at the service of even the least worthy who stand before us needing sympathy or help. If we have this feeling, we should look at no human life with disdain. It will put an end to all our miserable pride, to all our petty tyrannies and despotisms. It will lead us to ask concerning every one who passes before us, not, "What can I get from this man for my own gain? How can I make him serve me?" but rather, "What can I do to help this brother of mine, to add to his happiness, to relieve his trouble, to put him in the way of successful life, to comfort his sorrow, and to give him pleasure?"

If this were the habitual attitude of love, paradise would soon be restored. We live continually in the midst of great human needs, and every one has something to give, something that would help a little, at least, in supplying these needs. If we have but our five barley loaves, and bring them to our Master for his blessing, we can go forth and with them feed thousands.

Then we need not fear that in giving out our paltry store we shall impoverish ourselves. No, it is by selfishly withholding our little that impoverishment will come to us. Had the woman refused to feed the hungry stranger at her gate, her meal and oil would have sufficed for only one little day for herself and her son. But she recognized her scanty supply; and, lo! it lasted for them both through all the day of the famine. If we use what we have for ourselves alone, it will waste and soon be done, and we shall starve. But if we pay our debt of love, and share our little, it will multiply, and will last unto the end. Ida Whipple Benham writes:—

> "Keep it not idly by thee—hoard it not!
> Thy friend hath need of it; behold, he stands
> Waiting to take the bounty of thy hands;
> Pay him the debt thou owest, long forgot,

Or—hast thou paid already—ease his lot
Of that which he would sell, or loaf, or lands—
Whate'er his need can spare and thine demands;
So shall thy wealth be clean and without spot

Dost thou not know? Hast thou not understood?
The stagnant pool breeds pestilence, disease;
The hurrying stream bears bounty on its tide.
Pass on thy gold, a messenger of good;
Swift let it speed on gracious ministries;
Wing it with love and let its flight be wide."

Chapter 7

The Responsibility of Greatness

"The easy path in the lowland hath little of grand or new,
But a toilsome ascent leads on to a wide and glorious view;
Peopled and warm is the valley, lonely and chill the height;
But the peak that is nearer the storm-cloud is nearer the stars of light."

No doubt it is natural to desire easy ways in life. None of us love hardness for its own sake. We all like to have good things come to us as favors, as gifts, without toil or sacrifice or cost. But not thus, ordinarily, do life's best things come to us. Nor would they be best things if we received them in this way. The gold of life we must dig out of the rocks with our own hands in order to make it our own. The larger blessing we find not in the possessing, but in the getting. This is the secret that lies at the heart of our Lord's beatitude, "It is more blessed to give than to receive." He did not say it is more pleasant to give than to receive, or more easy to human nature, but more blessed.

It is related in an ancient Bible record that the people of Joseph came once to Joshua with a complaint concerning their allotment in the promised land. They said, "Why hast thou given me but one lot and one part for an inheritance, seeing I am great people?" Joshua's answer was, "If thou be a great people, get thee up to the forest, and cut down for thyself there." The incident is full of suggestion. It gives us an example of a premise with two different conclusions. The people said, "We are a great tribe; therefore give us a larger portion." Joshua said, "Yes, you are a great people; therefore, clear the forests from the mountains, drive out the enemy, and take possession." To his mind, their greatness was a reason why they should take care of themselves and win their own larger portion.

One teaching from this incident is that it is not the bravest and most wholesome thing to be eager for favors and for help from others. These people wished to be recognized as the most important tribe, but they wanted this prominence and wealth bestowed upon them without exertion of their own. There are men of this class in every community. They want to rise in the world, but they would rise on the exertions and sacrifices of others — not their own. They want larger farms, but they would have some other hand than their own clear away the forests and cultivate the soil.

We find the same in spiritual life. There are those who sigh for holiness and beauty of character, but they are not willing to pay the price. They sing, "More holiness give me," and dream of some lofty spiritual attainment, some transfiguration, but they are not willing to endure the toils, to fight the battles, and to make the self-sacrifices necessary to win these celestial heights. They would make praying a substitute for effort, for struggle, for the crucifying of self. They want a larger spiritual inheritance, but they have no thought of taking it in primeval forests which their own hands must cut down.

The truth is, however, that God gives us our inheritance just as he gave Joseph's lot to him. Our promised land has to be won, every inch of it. And each must win his own personal portion. No one can win the inheritance for any other. You must conquer your own temptations — your dearest friend by your side cannot overcome them for you. You must train and discipline your own faith. You must cultivate your own heart-life. You must learn patience, gentleness, and all the lessons of love for yourself. No one can give you any Christian grace as one gives a present to another. There is a deep truth in that touch in the parable, when the wise virgins refused to give of their oil to those whose lamps were going out. Perhaps you have thought it ungenerous in them, when you heard them say, "Go to them that sell, and buy for yourselves. We have not enough for us and you." But the teaching is that grace is not transferable, cannot be passed from heart to heart. The wise could not give of their oil to the foolish. No one can live for another at any point. Even God cannot give us holiness, peace, and the rich results of victorious living, without struggle, battle, or self-denial upon our own part. True it is that God works in us both to will and to do, but the text which tells us this begins, "Work out your own salvation." God works in us only when we begin to work at his bidding.

Another lesson here is that truest friendship must ofttimes decline to do for men what they can do for themselves. Joshua may have seemed a little unkind to his own tribe, but really he was not. The best kindness to them was to send them out to do the things they could do. It was far better to command them to go into the forest and cut down the timber and clear off the land for themselves, than it would have been to give them a broad acreage of new land all cleared and under cultivation. It was far better to send them to drive out the enemies with the iron chariots, conquering the valley for themselves, than it would have been to send an army to make the conquest for them.

Our best friends are not those who make life easy for us; our best friends are those who put courage, energy, and resolution into our hearts. There are thousands of lives dwarfed and hurt irreparably by pampering. Parents, ofttimes, in the very warmth and eagerness of their love, do sad harm in their children's lives by overhelping them; by doing things for them which it were better to teach them to do for themselves; by sparing them struggles, self-denials, hardships, which it were better for the children to meet.

Friendship is in constant danger of overhelping in this way. When one we love comes to us with a difficulty, it is love's first impulse to solve it for himself. If you can wake up a young man, arouse his sleeping or undiscovered powers, so that he will win a fortune or do a brave thing with his own hands and brain, that is an infinitely better thing to do for him than if you were to give him a fortune as a present. In the former case, in getting his fortune, he has gotten also trained powers, energy, strength, self-reliance, disciplined character, and all the elements that belong to strong manhood. In the other case he has gotten nothing but the money. He has missed all the lessons he would have learned, and all the enlargement and enrichment of life he would have gotten in the struggle and the conquest, and these are the true acquisitions in life. Things are not possessions. Money and real estate and stocks and bonds are not real possessions in the hands of a man with a soul. They are entirely external to the man himself. They make a man no greater, no more a man, if they are merely put into his hands. In winning a fortune the man will grow. Work itself is always a better blessing than that which one works to get. Hence it is a greater kindness to incite another to open the hard rocks and thus find the water for himself, than it is to bring him the water which another has led down from the mountains.

That was the way Joshua showed his friendship for these children of Joseph. He would not do them the unkindness of freeing them from the toil of conquest and subjugation. He set them to win the land for themselves, because the blessing lay as much in the winning as in the possessing.

That is God's way with us. He does not make life easy for us. He does not promise to lift the burden off our shoulder even when we cast it upon him. It is God's gift to us, this burden of ours, and to lay it down would be to lay down a blessing. It is something our life needs, and it would be an unkindness to take it away. Surely it is a wiser love that put new strength into your heart and arm, so that you can go on with your hard duty, your heavy responsibility, your weight of care, without fainting, than would be the love which should take the load away and leave you free from any burden. You may think you would prefer the latter way, that it would be easier, but you would miss the blessing, and your life would be weaker and poorer in the end.

God's purpose always is to make something of us, to bring out the best that is in us. Hence he does not clear the forest for us, but puts the axe into our hands and bids us to cut it down for ourselves. And while we prepare the ground for tillage we grow healthy and strong ourselves through the toil. He does not drive out the enemies for us; he puts the sword into our hands and sends us to drive them out. The struggle does us good. The wrestling makes us strong.

Still another lesson from this incident is that true greatness should show itself, not in demanding favors or privileges, but in achieving great things. The people of Joseph thought that their prominence entitled them to a portion above others. "No," said Joshua, "your prominence entitles you only to the privilege of the finest heroism and the largest labor." So he gave them the hardest task. The way a commander honors the best regiment on the field is not be assigning it to some easy post, to some duty away from danger. He honors it by giving it the most perilous post, the duty requiring the most splendid courage. So it is in all life — the place of honor is always the hardest place, where the most delicate and difficult duty must be done, where the heaviest burden of responsibility must be borne. It is never a real honor to be given an easy place. Instead of demanding a place of honor as a favor of friendship, which sets no seal of greatness upon our brow, we should win our place of honor by worthy deeds and services.

Our Lord taught this lesson when the disciples strove for the highest positions. They wished that he would merely appoint them to seats on his right and left hand. His answer is very important. Men are not appointed to the high places in spiritual life, he said, "It is not mine to give." Even Christ cannot give any disciple rank or place in his kingdom. It must be won by the disciple himself. In human governments, rulers may put their favorites in places of honor merely to show them regard. Appointments are ofttimes arbitrary in such cases, and unworthy men are set in exalted seats. But places are never given to men in Christ's kingdom; they must be won.

Then our Lord went further and explained the principle on which places are assigned to his disciples. "Whosoever would become great among you shall be your minister; and whosoever would be first among you shall be your servant." That is, rank in Christ's kingdom is in proportion to service. He who serves his fellow-men most utterly, in Christ's name, is the highest among men. Or, to put it in another form, instead of claiming rank by appointment or favor, you must win it by serving your fellows, by using your strength, your abilities, your greatness, in doing good to others. The only privilege your superiority over others gives you is the privilege of doing good to others in superior ways.

This truth is far-reaching in its applications. It should sweep out of our thought forever all feeling that others owe us favors; all that spirit which shows itself in self-seeking, in claims for place or precedence over others. It should make us despise all the miserable toggery of professed rank, aristocracy, blood, in which so many people play such farces. "What are you doing with your life?" is the only question that is asked, when rank is to be measured. The law of love is that with whatsoever we have we must serve our fellowmen. Selfishness discrowns a life. The least talented man in the world who uses his little powers with which to serve and help others, is higher in rank in God's sight than the most nobly gifted man who uses his great power only to advance his own interests.

The most highly dowered life that this world ever saw was that of Jesus Christ. Yet he demanded no recognition of men. He claimed no rank. He never said his lowly place was too small, too narrow, for the exercise of his great abilities. He used his greatness in doing good, in blessing the world. He washed men's feet with those hands which angels would have kissed. He was the greatest among men, and he was the servant of all. That is the true mission of greatness — to serve. There is no other worthy way of using whatever gifts God has bestowed upon us. Instead of claiming place, distinction, rank, position, and attention, because of our gifts, abilities, wisdom, or name, we must use all we have to bless the world and to honor God.

Chapter 8

The Ability of Faith

"Nay, never falter; no great deed is done
By falterers who ask for certainty.
No good is certain but the steadfast mind.
The undivided will to seek the good;
'Tis that compels the elements and wrings
A human music from the indifferent air.
The greatest gift the hero leaves his race
Is to have been a hero. Say we fall!
We deed the high tradition of the world,
And leave our spirit in our children's breast."
~James Russell Lowell

Because a thing is hard is no reason why we should not do it. The limit of duty is not the limit of human ability. We ought to do many things which, with our own strength alone, we cannot do. There is a realm of faith in which a Christian should live which is not under the sway of natural laws. The religion of Christ counts for little with us if it does not enable us to do more than others who know not its secret. Our righteousness must exceed the righteousness of the scribes and Pharisees. Our achievements and attainments must be of a higher order then those of this world's people. The true spirit of Christian faith is one of quiet confidence in the presence of any duty, any requirement. It knows no impossibilities. It staggers at no command. It shrinks from no responsibility. It is crushed under no burden.

"So nigh is grandeur to our dust,
So near is God to man,
When duty whispers low, "Thou must,"
The youth replies, "I can!"

Two brothers came to the Master with a request that they might have the first place in his kingdom. They were thinking of earthly rank. The Master answered by asking them if they were able to accept his cup and baptism. They did not know what he meant, but they believed so utterly in him that they calmly answered, "We are able."

This was a committal from which there could be no withdrawal. It implied courage. They knew not to what future they were going; what it would cost them to be true to their pledge; but they faltered not. It implied love for their Master. This was the secret of it all. They could not be separated from him. They would follow him anywhere, they loved him so. It implied faith. They did not know what the cup would be which they had solemnly promised to drink; but they believed in Christ, and in his love and wisdom, and were sure he would lead them only to what would be the truest and the best for them.

This is the lesson every follower of Christ should learn. To every call of the Master, to every allotment of duty, to every assignment of service, to every laying of the cross at our feet, to every requirement that he makes of us, our answer should be, "We are able." This is easy enough so long as only pleasant things are asked of us; but pleasant things do not test discipleship. We must be ready to say it when our expectation of honor in following Christ is suddenly dashed away and dishonor appears in its place, and when it means the lifting of the dark cross upon our shoulders and bearing it after him.

Hence the answer of all noble life to every call of duty is, "I am able." The question of ability is not to be considered. God never asks us to do any thing we cannot do through the strength which he is ready also to give. It is thus that God's men have always answered God's calls. "Here am I," was the formula in the Old Testament times. Thus patriarchs and prophets and messengers responded when they heard the divine voice calling their names. There was not hesitation. They did not linger to question their fitness or their ability. In New Testament days we find the same obedience. St. Paul is a noble illustration. It would seem that the motto of his life was, "I am ready." That was what he always said, whatever the divine bidding. He was forewarned of chains at Jerusalem, and his friends begged him not to go. But his answer was, "I am ready not to be bound only, but also to die at Jerusalem for the name of the Lord Jesus." Again, he was thinking of Rome, that great metropolis of the heathen world, the center of the world's power and splendor, and he wrote, "I am ready to preach the gospel to you that are at Rome also; for I am not ashamed of the gospel of Christ." He is in a dungeon, a prisoner of Christ, knowing that he will soon die as a martyr, and he writes to a friend, "I am ready to be offered."

An old missionary seal bore the representation of an ox standing between a plough and an altar, with the legend, "Ready for either." The meaning was that the missionary of Christ must be ready either for toil and service, or for sacrifice on the alter, if that should be the Lord's will. That was the spirit of St. Paul. He was ready for life, if Christ so willed; for life to the very extreme of self-denying, selfconsuming service, if that were the call; for life in chains and in dungeons, if the Master led him to such sufferings. Or, he was ready for death, if by dying he could best glorify his Lord. This is the only true spirit of one who would follow Christ faithfully and fully. Whatever the call of the Master may be, the instant answer of the servant should be, "I am ready. I am able."

There are many things in Christian duty which, if our little human strength were all we could command, would be impossibilities. Our Lord sent out his disciples to heal the sick and to raise the dead. They could do neither of these things, and they might have said, "We cannot cure fevers, nor open blind eyes, nor make lame men walk, nor restore the breath of life to the dead." Instead of saying this, however, their reply really was, "We are able;" and as they spoke in the name of Christ, power was in their words and in their touch, and miracles were wrought by them. St Paul has a remarkable word which illustrates the same truth. He is speaking of the endurance of hardships. "I have learned," he says, "in whatsoever state I am, therein to be content." Then a little farther on he says, "I can do all things in him that strengtheneth me." Here we have the confidant 'I am able," with its secret laid bare — "in him that strengtheneth me.

This is the law of Christ's kingdom. Nothing is impossible with God. When he gives us a duty, he will give the strength we need to do it. When he sends one of his servants on an errand, he is ready to give power to perform the task, however hard it may be. When there is a battle to fight, he will inspire the heart and nerve the arm to fight it, so that we may become "more than conquerors through him that loved us." We are ever strongest when we are weakest in ourselves, because the measure of our conscious weakness is the measure of the strength he imparts to us. This is a blessed secret. It puts the very power of God within our reach. We can do all things in Christ.

There are but two conditions — obedience and faith. The strength will not be give unless we obey. We must not wait to have it given before we will set out — it will not be given at all if we do this. Not matter how difficult, how seemingly impossible, the duty may be, we must instantly obey, or no power will be forthcoming. It is when we go forward confidently in the way of duty that the strength is given. There must also be faith. We cannot do these things ourselves; there is not sufficient strength is us. But when we, without doubting, begin to do God's will, he will put his strength into us. Thus, whatever the task he gives, we may say with quiet confidence, "We are able." Whatever burden he lays upon us, we need not falter, nor fear to try to bear it. There is no divine promise that the burden will be lifted away, but there is an assurance that we shall be sustained as we walk in faith beneath it.

But this sustaining comes not to him who falters and hesitates; it comes to him only who goes forward firmly in the way marked out for him. It comes not to him who waits for the opening of the way before he will set out; the way will open only to the feet of him who goes on unflinchingly and unquestioningly in obedience to the call of duty, regardless of high walls or shut gates or overflowing rivers crossing his path. The floods of the Jordan were not cut off while the pilgrim host lay back in their camps, nor while they were moving down the green banks, nor even while they tarried close to the brink, waiting for a way to be made for them. It was not until the feet of the priests who led the host, moving firmly on, trod the very edge of the water, that the river opened to allow them to pass through to the land of promise. It never would have opened to feet that waited on the band for it to open. It is so in all cases. There is a time for quiet, patient waiting — when we have done all we can. But there is a time when waiting is defeat and failure.

To none of us, if we are living earnestly can life be easy. Duties are too large for our ability. Circumstances are hard. Our condition has its uncongenialities. Our tasks are more than our hands can perform. We are disposed to fret and to be discontented, and then to be discouraged, and to say we cannot live sweetly and beautifully where our lot is set. But this is never true. Difficulty never makes impossibility when we have the power of Christ from which to draw. No duties then are ever too large. No burdens are ever too heavy. There is not environment in which we cannot live patiently and sweetly.

It is in the hard lot that we learn our best lessons, and do our best living. Certain birds, when they are to be taught to sing new songs, are shut up in a darkened cage. Then they are caused to hear in the darkness the sweet strains which they are to learn.

By and by they begin to sing what they hear, and they are kept singing it over and over until they have fully learned it. Then the curtain is withdrawn, and now they sing the sweet songs in the sunshine. It is thus that God puts us sometimes into darkness where the conditions are hard. "How can we sing the Lord's songs here?" we ask. But divine help comes to us, and grace, and as we try to live gently, patiently, and lovingly, and to sing the songs of joy, we find we can do it in Christ who strengtheneth us. Then there is always blessing in victoriousness. However great the cost of noble living may be, the reward is always greater than the cost.

> "How very hard it is to be
> A Christian! Hard for you and me,—
> Not the mere task of making real
> That duty up to its ideal,
> Effecting thus, complete and whole,
> A purpose of the human soul—
> For that is always, hard to do;
> But hard, I mean, for me and you
> To realize it more or less,
> With even the moderate success
> Which commonly repays our strife
> To carry out the aims of life.
> 'Tis aim is greater,' you will say,
> 'And so more arduous in every way;'
> But the importance of their fruits
> Still proves to man, in all pursuits,
> Proportional encouragement."

Let us never disappoint God by saying in any place that we cannot live there beautifully. Let us rather accept the hardship, the struggles, the burden, the trying environment; and, helped by the divine Spirit, let us learn to do always the things that please God. "When we acquiesce in a trouble," says Fenelon, "it is no longer such." Submission takes the bitterness out of pain, which becomes calamity when we resist and chafe. "Peace in this life springs from acquiescence even in disagreeable things, not from exemption from bearing them." Acquiescence is the faith that gets the divine strength which makes all things possible.

Chapter 9

Sources of Strength

"O how many hearts are breaking!
O how many hearts are aching
For a loving touch and token,
For the word you might have spoken."
~Josephine Pollard.

"God doth suffice! O thou, the patient one,
Who puttest faith in him, and none beside,
Bear thou thy load; under the setting sun
The glad tents gleam: thou wilt be satisfied."

We all need help. None of us are sufficient in ourselves for all the exigencies of our condition. Life is too large for any of us. Its duties are too great for strength. Its trials overtax our power of endurance. Its antagonisms over master us. Our own hearts contain only a little cupful of oil; and, unless we can replenish them from some reserve supply, our lamps will go out, leaving us in darkness.

Yet we are required to meet life victoriously. We are not to succumb to its stress or struggle. We are told that while our temptations are far more than a match for our strength, yet we need not fall in them. The task is set for us of being more than conquerors in all life's trials. We are not to be crushed by sorrow. We are to rejoice always, though always enduring sore grief.

It is possible, therefore, for us to receive help from without our own little life, to make us equal to whatever we may have to bear or to endure. It is important that we learn how to live so that we can get this help. What are the sources from which we may draw strength in our time of need? Evidently they are twofold. We can be helped in a certain way by human hands; and we can be helped in the largest measure we need by the divine strength.

In all things the life of Christ is our pattern. He lived a human life to show us how to live. He did not meet life otherwise than we must meet it. He wrought no miracles to make trials easier for himself than they would be for his followers. In our Lord's experience in Gethsemane we have an illustration of the way he sought help in time of great need, both from the human and the divine source.

The real agony of Christ's atoning death was in Gethsemane, and not on Calvary. It was there he fought the battle and won the victory. After this there was no more struggle. It is worth our while to look closely into our Lord's experiences in the Garden, to learn the secrets of the victory he won there. It will be ours some time to face a sore struggle, a bitter disappointment, a great trial, a keen sorrow, or to take up a heavy cross. How can we prepare ourselves for the experience, so as to meet it victoriously?

The Mexicans whisper over the cradle of a new-born babe, "Child, thou art born to suffer; endure and hold thy peace! Courage in meeting trial is good. We should learn to take up our burden quietly and walk beneath it steadfastly. We should learn to endure and hold our peace. There are men who do this, hardening themselves against pain and sorrow, and meeting life's misfortunes and trials stoically, with solemn firmness. But this is not the best way to meet life. It was not thus that our Lord met his trials. He did not go to his cross stoically. True, he set himself to endure and hold his peace. Never, before or since, has anguish been borne so victoriously, or has the world seen such peace as filled the Redeemer's soul during all the hours of his deepest humiliation. But his was not the peace of stoical hardening; it was the peace of God which kept his heart and mind.

"Endure and hold thy peace" is not all of the lesson. There is something better than stoicism. We need not struggle unaided. It is not a mark of weakness to accept help in hours of great need. Jesus desired to be sustained as he entered his agony. First, he craved and sought the help of human sympathy. It seems strange to us, at first thought, that he, the strong Son of God, could receive help from men. And from such men as his disciples were. It showed his true humanity. It showed, too, how real human friendship was to him. We know that his friends received help and comfort from him, but we are not so apt to think of him needing them and receiving strength from their love. But here we see him leaning upon them, wanting them near to him while he struggled and suffered, and craving their sympathy and tenderness. How sad it was, then, that the three chosen disciples whom he lead into the depths of the Garden that they might watch with him and strengthen him by their love, slept instead of watching!

In Brittany, among the peasants, they have this beautiful legend of the robin. They say that when the Saviour moved toward Calvary, bearing his cross, with enemies all about him, a robin hovered near. And, reckless of the tumult, the bird flew down and snatched a cruel thorn from the Christ's bleeding forehead. Then over the robin's bosom flowed the sacred blood, tinting with its ruby stream the bird's brown plumage. This, the peasants say, was the origin of the red spot on the robin's breast.

"And evermore the sweet bird bore upon its tender breast
The warm hue of the Saviour's blood, a shinning seal impressed.
Hence, dearest to the peasant's heart, 'mid birds of grove and plain,
They hold the robin, which essayed to soothe the Saviour's pain."

This is only a legend. No bird plucked a thorn from that sacred brow. Not by even so small a soothing was the Saviour' anguish that day mitigated. Yet it was in the power of his disciples to have soothed his bitter agony immeasurably. But when he came back to them after each struggle, hoping to find comfort from their love, they were asleep. They failed him, not through carelessness, but through faintness. The spirit was willing, but the flesh was weak. Had they been stronger, it would have been a little easier for Christ to endure the cross. Their love would have taken at least one thorn from his crown of thorns.

We all need human friendship. We need it specially in our times of darkness. He does not well, he lives not wisely, who in the days of prosperity neglects to gather about his life a few loving friends, who will be a strength to him in the days of stress and need.

Then we should be ready, too, to give the strength of our love to those whom we see passing into the ways of struggle of sorrow. We should not commit the mistake of our Lord's friends, failing those who need and expect our cheer. There is a deep lesson in the words Christ spoke at the last to the men to whom he had come three times in vain, craving sympathy. "Sleep on now, and take your rest; it is enough, the hour is come." There was no need, then, for longer watching, nor could any good come of it. The struggle was over, the victory had been won without them, and there was nothing left for them to do.

This experience is too common. Continually men close beside us are needing sympathy and love which we have it in our power to give, but which we do not give, letting them pass on unhelped. Here in a stanza is told too many a life-story:—

"A heart beat in our midst that vainly tried
Companionship of other hearts to gain;
A soul lived pure and sweet before our eyes,
Whom our unsympathy caused cruel pain."

There is a time to show sympathy, when it is golden; when this time has passed, and we have only slept meanwhile, we may as well sleep on. You did not go near your friend when he was fighting his battle alone. You might have helped him then. What use is there in your coming to him now, when he has conquered without your aid? You paid no attention to your neighbor when he was bending under life's loads, and struggling with difficulties, obstacles, and adversities. You let him alone then. You never told him that you sympathized with him. You never said a brave, strong word of cheer to him in those days. You never scattered even handful of flowers on his hard path. Now that he is dead and lying in his coffin, what is the use in your standing beside his still form, and telling the people how nobly he battled, how heroically he lived; and speaking words of commendation? No, no; having let him go on, unhelped, uncheered, unencouraged, through the days when he needed so sorely your warm sympathy, and craved so hungrily your cheer, you may as well sleep on and take your rest, letting him alone unto the end. Nothing can be done now. Too laggard are the feet that come with comfort when the time for giving comfort is past.

"Ah! Woe for the word that is never said
Till the ear is deaf to hear;
And woe for the lack to the fainting head
Of the ringing shout of cheer;
Ah! Woe for the laggard feet that tread
In the mournful wake of the bier.

A pitiful thing the gift to-day
That is dross and nothing worth,
Though if it had come but yesterday,
It had brimmed with sweet the earth;
A fading rose in a death-cold hand,
That perished in want and dearth."

Shall we not take our lesson from the legend of the robin that plucked a thorn from the Saviour's brow, and thus sought to lesson his pain rather than from the story of the disciples, who slept and failed to give the help which the Lord sought from their love?

Thus can we strengthen those whose burden are heavy, and whose struggles and sorrows are sore.

So much for the human help. There was another source of help in our Lord's Garden experience. If there had not been, he would have been utterly unhelped in all his sore need, for human friendship proved inadequate. "Being in an agony, he prayed." He sought strength from heaven. He crept to his Father's feet and made supplication to him and was heard.

As we watch him in his struggle, we see that he grows calmer and quieter as he prays. It is evident that divine help comes to him. He is sustained and strengthened. At length, when he comes from his pleading, his heart is at rest; his pleading has died away in the sweetest and divinest of peace.

We have the same infinite and unfailing source of help in our times of great need. Human friendship can go with us a little way, yet not into the inner depths of our experience of sorrow or trial. Human sympathy is very sweet, but it is weak, and ofttimes sleeps when we most need its cheer and comfort. But when the human ceases to avail, the divine is ready. In the face of life's great needs, when no other help can come to us, God comes, and from his divine fullness gives all that we need.

The prayer of our Lord in the Garden is a model for all who would find help in sore need. It was intense in its pleading, but it also breathed the most perfect submission, "Not my will, but thine be done." No other spirit of prayer is pleasing to God, or bring blessing. The answer did not come, the cup did not pass away, and yet our Lord was really strengthened and helped in his praying. At its close, he came forth with peace in his heart, ready now to pass into the darkness of his cross.

'How was he helped," some one may ask, "when that which he craved was not granted?" He was not spared the sorrow, but he was strengthened to endure it. This is God's way in much of our praying. We do not know what would be a blessing to us. What to our thoughts seems bread, might really be a stone to us. We may make our requests for things we desire, but we should make them humbly and submissively. If it is not our Father's will to grant us what we wish, he gives us grace to go without it. If he does not avert the trial from which we ask to be spared, he strengthens us for meeting it. Thus no true prayer ever goes unanswered. The divine help never fails. There is a limit to what our human friends can do for us: but God is infinite, and all his strength is ready to our hand, to help us as we need.

Chapter 10

The Blessing of Weakness

"No drop but serves the slowly lifting tide,
No dew but has an errand to some flower,
No smallest star but sheds some helpful ray."

We are not accustomed to think of weakness as a condition of blessing. We would say, "Blessed is strength. Blessed are the strong." But Bible beatitudes are usually the reverse of what nature would say. "Blessed are the meek." "Blessed are ye when men shall reproach you." The law of the cross lies deep in spiritual life. It is by the crucifying of the flesh that the spirit grows into beauty. So, "Blessed are the weak, for they shall have God's strength, " is a true scriptural beatitude, although its very words are not found in the Bible.

Weakness is blessed because it insures to us more of the sympathy and help of Christ. Weakness ever appeals to a gentle heart. We see illustrations of this truth in our common human life. What can be more weak and helpless than blindness? Here is a blind child in a home. Her condition seems pitiable. She gropes about in darkness. She is unaware of dangers that may beset her, and cannot shield herself from any harm that threatens her. The windows through which others see the world to her are closed, and she is shut up in darkness. She is almost utterly helpless. Yet her very weakness is her strength. It draws to itself the best love and help of the whole household. The mother's heart has no such tender thought for any of the other children as for the blind girl. The father carries her continually in his affection and is ever doing gentle things for her. Brothers and sisters strive in all ways to supply her lack. The result is that no other member of the family is sheltered so safely as she is, and that none is half so strong. Her very helplessness is the secret of her strength. Her closed eyes and outstretched hands and tottering feet appeal resistlessly to all who love her, inspiring them to thought and help, as do the strength and winning grace of no other one in the household.

This illustrates also the special divine thought and care for the weak. All the best things in human life are really hints and gleams of the divine life. The heart of Christ goes out in peculiar interest toward the weak. Paul could well afford to keep his "thorn" with its burdening weakness, because it made him far more the object of divine sympathy and help. So always weakness makes strong appeal to the divine compassion. We think of suffering or feebleness as a misfortune. It is not altogether so, however, if it makes us dearer and brings us nearer to the heart of Christ. Blessed is weakness, for it draws to itself the strength of God.

Weakness is blessed, also, because it saves from spiritual peril. St. Paul tells us that his "thorn" was given to him to keep him humble. Without it he would have been exalted over much and would have lost his spirituality. We do not know how much of his deep insight into the things of God, and his power in service for his Master, St. Paul owed to this torturing "thorn." It seemed to hinder him and it caused him incessant suffering, but it detained him in the low valley of humility, made him ever conscious of his own weakness and insufficiency, and thus kept him near to Christ whose home is with the humble.

Spiritual history is full of similar cases. Many of God's noblest servants have carried "thorns" in their flesh all their days, but meanwhile they have had spiritual blessing and enrichment which they never would have had if their cries for relief had been granted. We do not know what we owe to the sufferings of those who have gone before us. Prosperity has not enriched the world as adversity has done. The best thoughts, the richest life lessons, the sweetest songs that have come down to us from the past, have not come from lives that have known no privation, no adversity, but are the fruits of pain, of weakness, of trial. Men have cried out for emancipation from the bondage of hardship, of sickness, of infirmity, of self-denying necessity; not knowing that the thing which seemed to be hindering them in their career was the very making of whatever was noble, beautiful, and blessed in their life.

There are few people who have not some "thorn" rankling in their flesh. In one it is an infirmity of speech, in another an infirmity of sight, in another an infirmity of hearing. Or it may be lameness, or a disease, slow but incurable, or constitutional timidity, or excessive nervousness, or a disfiguring bodily deformity, or an infirmity of temper. Or it may be in one's home, which is cold, unloving, and uncongenial; or it may be in the life of a loved one — sorrow or moral failure; or it may be a bitter personal disappointment through untrue friendship or love inrequited. Who has not his "thorn"?

We should never forget that in one sense our "thorn" is a "messenger of Satan," who desires by it to hurt our life, to mar our peace, to spoil the divine beauty in us, to break our communion with Christ. On the other hand, however, Christ himself has a loving design in our "thorn." He wants it to be a blessing to us. He would have it keep us humble, save us from becoming vain; or he means it to soften our hearts and make us more gentle. He would have the uncongenial things in our environment discipline us into heavenly-mindedness, give us greater self-control, help us to keep our hearts loving and sweet amid harshness and unlovingness. He would have our pain teach us endurance and patience, and our sorrow and loss teach us faith.

That is, our "thorn" may either be a blessing to us, or it may do us irreparable harm — which, it depends upon ourselves. If we allow it to fret us; if we chafe, resist, and complain; if we lose faith and lose heart, it will spoil our life. But if we accept it in the faith that in its ugly burden it has a blessing for us; if we endure it patiently, submissively, unmurmuringly; if we seek grace to keep our heart gentle and true amid all the trial, temptation, and suffering it causes, it will work good, and out of its bitterness will come sweet fruit. The responsibility is ours, and we should so relate ourselves to our "thorn" and to Christ, that growth and good, not harm and marring, shall come to us from it. Such weakness is blessed only if we get the victory over it through faith in Christ.

There is a blessing in weakness, also, because it nourishes dependence on God. When we are strong, or deem ourselves strong, we are really weak, since then we trust in ourselves and do not seek divine help. But when we are consciously weak, knowing ourselves unequal to our duties and struggles, we are strong, because then we turn to God and get his strength. Too many people think their weakness a barrier to their usefulness, or make it an excuse for doing little with their life. Instead of this, however, if we give it to Christ, he will transform it into strength. He says his strength is made perfect in weakness; that is, what is wanting in human strength he fills and makes up with divine strength. St. Paul had learned this when he said he gloried now in his weaknesses, because on account of them the strength of Christ rested upon him, so that, when he was weak, then he was strong — strong with divine strength.

The people who have done the greatest good in the world, who have left the deepest, most abiding impression upon the lives of others, have not been those whom men called the strong. Much of the world's best work has been done by the weak, by those with broken lives. Successful men have piled up vast fortunes, established large enterprises, or won applause in some material way; but the real influence that has made the world better, enriched lives, taught men the lessons of love, and sweetened the springs of society, has come largely, not from the strong, but from the weak.

I walked over a meadow and the air was full of delicious fragrance. Yet I could see no flowers. There was tall grass waving on all sides, but the fragrance did not come from the grass. Then I parted the grass and looked beneath it, and there, close to the earth, hidden out of sight by the showy growths in the meadow, were multitudes of lowly little flowers. I had found the secret of the sweetness — it poured out from these humble hiding flowers. This is a picture of what is true everywhere in life. Not from the great, the conspicuous, the famed in any community, comes the fragrance which most sweetens the air, but from lowly lives, hidden, obscure, unpraised, which give out the aroma of unselfishness, of kindness, of gentleness. In many a home it is from the room of an invalid, a sufferer, that the sweetness comes which fills all the house. We know that it is from the cross of Christ that the hollowing influence flowed which all these centuries has been refining and enriching and softening the world's life. So it is always — out of weakness and suffering, and from crushed, broken lives, comes the blessing that renews and heals the world.

> "The healing of the world
> Is in its nameless saints."

We need only to make sure of one thing, what we do indeed bring our weakness to Christ and lean on him in simple faith. This is the vital link in getting the blessing. Weakness itself is a burden; it is chains upon our limbs. If we try to carry it alone we shall only fail. But if we lay it on the strong Son of God and let him carry us and our burden, going on quietly and firmly in the way of duty, he will make our very weakness a secret of strength. He will not take the weakness from us — that is not his promise — but he will so fill it with his own power that we shall be strong, more than conquerors, able to do all things through Christ who strengtheneth us.

It is a blessed secret — this of having our burdening weakness transformed into strength. The secret can be found only in Christ, but in him it can be found by every lowly, trusting disciple.

Chapter 11

Loving Victorioulsy

"I like the man who faces what he must
With step triumphant and a heart of cheer;
Who fights the daily battle without fear;
Sees his hopes fail, yet keeps unfaltering trust
That God is God; that, somehow, true and just,
His plans work out for mortals; not a tear
Is shed when fortune, which the world holds dear,
Falls from his grasp. Better, with love, a crust,
Than living in dishonor; envies not
Nor loses faith in man; but does his best,
Nor even murmurs at his humbler lot;
But with a smile and words of hope, gives zest
To every toiler. He alone is great
Who, by a life heroic, conquers fate."

"Sarah K. Bolton.

We ought not to allow ourselves to be beaten in living. It is the privilege and duty of every believer in Christ to live victoriously. No man can ever reach noble character without sore cost in pain and sacrifice. All that is beautiful and worthy in life must be won in struggle. The crowns are not put upon men's heads through the caprice or favoritism of any king; they are the reward of victorious achievement. We can make life easy, in a way, if we will, by shirking its battles, by refusing to grapple with its antagonisms; but in this way we never can make anything beautiful and worthy of our life. We may keep alongshore with our craft, never pushing out into deep waters; but then we shall never discover new worlds, not learn the secret of the sea. We may spare ourselves costly service and great sacrifices, by saving our own life from hardships, risks, and waste, but we shall miss the blessing which can come only through the losing of self. "No cross, no crown" is the law of spiritual attainment.

"He who hath never a conflict hath never a victor's palm,

And only the toilers know the sweetness of rest and Calm".

Therefore God really honors us when he sets us in places where we must struggle. He is then giving us an opportunity to win the best honors and the richest blessing. Yet he never makes life so hard for us, in any circumstances, that we cannot live victoriously through the help which he is ready to give.

This lesson applies to temptation. Not one of us can miss temptation, but we need never fail nor fall in it. Never yet was a child of God in any terrible conflict with the Evil One in which it was not possible for him to overcome. There is a wonderful word in one of St. Paul's Epistles which we should write in letters of gold on our chamber walls: "There hath not temptation taken you but such as man can bear: but God is faithful, who will not suffer you to be tempted above that ye are able; but will with the temptation make also the way for escape, that ye may be able to endure it."

These are sublime assurances. Not one need ever say, "I cannot endure this temptation, and must yield and fall." This is never true. We need never fail. Christ met the sorest temptations, but he was always victorious; and now this tried and all-conquering Christ is by our side as we meet and endure our temptations, and we cannot fail when he is with us. It is possible, too, for us so the meet temptations as to change them into blessings. A conquered sin becomes a new strength in our life. We are stronger because every conquest gives us a new spirit of life; the strength we have defeated becomes now part of our own power.

Victoriousness in speech is among the hardest of life's conquests. The words of St. James are true to common experience, when he says that the tongue is harder to tame than any kind of beast or birds or creeping things or things in the sea; indeed, that no man can tame it. Yet he does not say that we need not try to tame our tongue. On the other hand he counsels us to be slow to speak and slow to wrath. A Christian ought to learn to control his speech. The capacity for harm in angry words is appalling. No prayer should be oftener on our lips than that in the old psalm:—

> "Set a watch, O Lord, before my mouth;
> Keep the door of my lips."

The hasty word of an uncontrolled moment may leave sore wounding and pain in a gentle heart, may mar a sweet friendship, may set an innocent life on a career of evil. Then the hurt in him who speaks ungoverned words is scarcely less sore. The pain that quickly follows their utterance is terrible penalty for the sin. There is ofttimes a cost, too, in results, which is incalculable. Lives have been shadowed, down to their close, by words which fell in a single flash from unlocked lips. Moses was not the only man who has been shut out of a land of promise by reason of one unadvised word. It is better to suffer wrong in silence than to run the risk of speaking in the excitement of anger.

One writes: "A single word spoken under the influence of passion, or rashly and inconsiderately spoken, may prove a source of abiding pain and regret; but the suffering of an act of injustice, of wrong, or of unkindness, in a spirit of meekness and forbearance, never renders us unhappy. The remembrance of a sinful of even a hasty word is not infrequently the cause of very deep mortification. The reflection that our words betrayed a weakness, if not a lack of moral and spiritual balance, humiliates us. It is a wound to our self-respect, and the consciousness that the regret is now unavailing adds a sting to the pain. But in the feeling that in our exercise of the meekness and forbearance inspired by the love of Christ we went further than we were bound to go, is not often a cause of distress. In a clam review of the act we do not feel that we wronged ourselves by making too large a sacrifice, or that our failure to resent the injury and to attempt to retaliate was a mistake. Reason and conscience approve the course, and it is a source of satisfaction and comfort."

The lesson applies also to whatever in our environment makes life hard. Sometimes we find ourselves in places and conditions of living in which it seems impossible for us to grow into strength and beauty of character. This is true of many young people in the circumstances in which they are born, and in which they must grow up. They find about them the limitations of poverty. They cannot get the education they seem to need to fit them for anything better than the most ordinary career. They envy other young people who have so much better opportunities. But these limitations, which seem to make fine attainments impossible, ofttimes prove the very blessings through which nobleness is reached. Early hardship is the best school for training men. Not many of those who have risen to the best and truest success began in easy places.

Sometimes it is poor health that appears to make it impossible for one to live grandly, at least to do much in the world. But this is not an insuperable barrier. Many people who have been invalids all their life have grown into rare sweetness of spirit, and have lived in the world in a way to make it better, and to leave influences of blessing behind them when they went away. Many a "shut in " has made a narrow room and a chamber of pain the center of a heavenly life, whose benedictions have gone far and wide. At least, there is no condition of health in which one cannot live victoriously in one's spirit, if not physically. One can be brave, cheerful, accepting one's limitations, praising God in sickness and in pain, sure always that what God wills is best, and that he who sings his little song of joy and praise in his prison is pleasing God and blessing the world.

> "Let sunshine and gladness illumine thy face;
> 'Twill help some one else to 'keep sweet.'
> Do troubles oppress thee? Let God be thy stay;
> 'Tis easy to sigh, but 'tis better to pray;
> Thy sunshine will come in his own blessed way:
> So trustingly try to 'keep sweet.'"

Sometimes that which makes life hard is in one's own nature. Passions are strong; temper seems uncontrollable; the affections are imbittered so that meekness and gentleness appear to be impossible; or the disposition is soured so that one finds it hard to be loving and sweet. The fault may be in one's early training, or the unhappy temper may be an inheritance. None of us come into the world saints, and ofttimes there are tendencies in one's childhood home, or in one's early years which give the wrong bias to the life. A few years later one awakes to find the nature misshapen, distorted, with the unlovely elements prominent and dominant.

Must one necessarily go through life to the end thus marred, with disposition spoiled, quick tempered, with appetites and passions uncontrollable? Not at all. In all these things we may be "more than conquerors through Him that loved us." The grace of Christ can take the most unlovely life and change it into beauty. Saintliness is impossible to none, where the grace of God is allowed to work freely and thoroughly.

Many persons find in their own homes the greatest obstacle in the way of their becoming beautiful and gentle in life. Home ought to be the best place in the world in which to grow into Christlikeness. There all the influences should be inspiring and helpful. It ought to be easy to be sweet in home's sacredness. Everything good ought there to find encouragement and stimulus. All home training should be towards "whatsoever things are lovely." Home should be life's best school. What the conservatory is to the little plant or flower that finds warmth, good soil, and gently culture there, growing into sweet loveliness, home should be to the young life that is born into it, and grows up within its doors. But not all home-life is ideal. Not in all homes is it easy to live sweetly and beautifully. Sometimes the atmosphere is unfriendly, cold, cheerless, chilling. It is hard to keep the heart gently and kindly in the bitterness that creeps into home-life.

But no matter how sadly a home may fail in its love and helpfulness, how much there may be in it of sharpness and bitterness, it is the mission of a Christian always to be sweet, to seek to overcome the hardness, to live victoriously. This is possible, too, through the help of Christ.

These are only illustrations of this lesson. Many of us find ourselves in uncongenial conditions in which we must stay, at least for the time. But, whatever the circumstances, we may live Christianly. God will never allow us to be put in any place in which, though the help of his grace, we cannot be good and beautiful Christians. Limitations, if we rightly use them, only help to make our life more earnest, more beautiful. A writer calls attention to the fact that every musical string is musical because it is tied at both ends and must vibrate in limited measure of distance. Cut the string, and let it fly loose, and it no more gives out musical notes. Its musicalness depends upon its limitations. So it is with many human lives; they become capable of giving out sweet notes only when they are compelled to move in restraint. The very hardness in their condition is that which brings out the best qualities in them, and produces the finest results in character and achievement.

This lesson applies also to experiences of misfortune, adversity, sorrow. Paul speaks of himself in one place as "sorrowful, yet always rejoicing." His life could not be crushed, his joy could not be quenched, his songs could not be hushed. We must all meet trial in some form, but one need never be overwhelmed by it. Yet it is very important that we should learn to pass through our sorrow as Christians. Do we meet it victoriously? We cannot help weeping; Jesus wept, and tears are sacred when love for our friends and love for Christ mingle in them. But our tears must not be rebellious. 'Thy will be done" must breathe through all our sobbings and cries, like the melody of a sweet song in a dark night of storm.

"Then sorrow whispered gently: 'Take
This burden up. Be not afraid;

An hour is short. Thou scarce wilt wake
To consciousness that I have laid
My hand upon thee, when the hour
Shall all have passed; and gladder than
For the brief pain's uplifting power,
Thou shalt but pity griefless men.'"

Sorrow hurts some lives. It imbitters them. It leaves them broken, disheartened, not caring more for life. But this is not the Christian way. We should accept sorrow, however it may come to us, as bringing with it a fragment of God's sweet will for us, as bringing also some new reveling of divine love. We should meet it quietly, reverently, careful not to miss the blessing it brings to us. Then we should rise up again at once and go on with our work and duty. Some hands are left hanging down after grief has come. "I do not care any more for life," men are sometimes heard to say. "I have no interest in my business, since my wife died. I want to give it all up." But that is not victorious living. Sorrow absolves us from no duty, from no responsibility. Our work is not finished because our friend's work is done. God's plan for our life goes on, though for the life dearest to us it has ended. We rise the morning after the funeral and find the old tasks waiting for us, clamoring for our coming, and must go forth at once to take them up. "Let us dry our tears and go on," wrote a Christian man to his friend, after a sore bereavement. That is the true spirit.

We ought to live more earnestly than ever after grief has touched our heart. Our life has been enriched by the experience. Tears leave the soil of the heart more fertile. The experience of sorrow teaches us many lessons. We are wise afterward, more thoughtful, better fitted to be guide and helper to others prepared especially to be comforters of those — whom, after our own experience, we find passing through affliction. Instead, therefore, of letting our hands hang down in despairing weakness, we should rise up quickly, fresh from our new anointing, and hasten on to the duty that waits for us.

Thus all Christian life should be victorious. We should never allow ourselves to be defeated in any experience that may come to us. With Christ to help us, we need never fail, but may ever be more than conquerors. Even the things that seem to be failures and defeats in our lives through the love and grace of Christ — if only we are faithful — will prove in the end to be successes and victories. Many a good man fails in a worldly sense, and yet in the moral and spiritual realm is more than conqueror. There is no real failure but in sin. Faithfulness to Christ is victory, even when all is lost.

"All things fulfil their purpose, low or high:
There is no failure; death can never mar
The lest or greatest of the things that are;
Until our work is done, it matters not how nigh
May be the night time that is never far,
That long ere sunset lights the evening star,
That throws its still shadow up into the sky.
To-day shall end what yesterday begun;
What we are planning others yet may build;
The leaves may wither, but the tree shall grow;
And though, at last, we leave our work undone,
Our life will not the less be all fulfilled;
Our work will all be even finished so,"

Chapter 12

Interpreters for God

"O Earth! Thou hast not any wind that blows
Which is not music; every weed of thine
Pressed rightly flows in aromatic wine.
And every humble hedge-row flower that grows,
And every little brown bird that doth sing,
Hath something greater than itself, and bears
A living word to every living thing,
Albeit it hold the message unawares."

God wants interpreters. He does not walk the earth in form that we can see, or speak to us in words that we can hear. Yet he is always with us, and he is always speaking to us. Once he sent his only begotten Son, and men saw his face — a face like their own, and heard his voice, a voice like their own. Now he has many sons; and in all of these, just in the measure in which they are true, God's face beams its love upon the world, and God's voice speaks its message to the world.

Every one of us has something to do in interpreting God to men. If we are his friends, the "secret of the Lord" is with us. Not a secret, however, which we are to keep to ourselves, but one which it is ours to declare. We are in the world to reveal God, and to make God's words plain to others.

We have many illustrations of this in the Scriptures. For example, twice in the story of Joseph do we find him acting as an interpreter for God. Two of his fellow-prisoners had dreams. Joseph told them the meaning of the dreams. Pharaoh had a dream which Egypt's wise men could not interpret, and Joseph was brought from his prison to tell its meaning. In both these cases the dreams were words of God, whose interpretation it was important to learn. In the case of the prisoners, the dreams were forecastings of the future of the two men. In the case of Pharaoh, they were revealings which the king needed to understand, in order that he might make provision for his people in the famine that was coming. It would have been a great calamity for Egypt and for the world if he had not learned the meaning of what God had spoken in his ear in the visions of the night. But without an interpreter he never could have known.

So we all stand in this world amid mysterious writings which we cannot read, having our dreams and visions, whose meanings we cannot ourselves interpret. Yet these writings and these visions are really God's words to us, divine teachings which we ought to understand, whose meanings it is intended we should find out. They have their lessons for us, which we need to know. They hold messages of comfort for our sorrows, of guidance for our dark paths, of instruction for our ignorance, of salvation for our perishing souls. We cannot live as we should live until we learn the meaning of these divine words. We need interpreters.

Take the little child. It comes into the world knowing nothing. On all sides are wonderful things — in nature, in its own life, in other lives, in books, in art, in providence. But the writings are all mysterious. The child understands nothing. Yet it is here to learn all it can of these writings. They are words of God which concern its own welfare. The child needs interpreters. And we are all only children of various growths. Life is full of enigmas for us. We bend over the Bible and find texts we cannot understand. There are mysteries in providence; they come into every life at some time. Yet in these obscure texts and these dark providences there are words of God hidden, words of love, of wisdom, of mercy. We all need interpreters to read off for us the mysterious handwriting of God.

Then it is our office as Christians to be interpreters for others. Joseph found the two prisoners sad, and his heart was touched with sympathy. He became eager to comfort them. This revealed the true and noble spirit in him. He had a warm, gentle heart. No one can ever be greatly useful in this world who does not enter into the world's experiences of need. Christ was moved with compassion when he saw human pain and sin. At once his love went out toward the sufferer, and he desired to impart help. Wherever we go we see sad faces which tell of unrest, of broken peace, of unsatisfied longings, of unanswered questions, of deep heart hungering. Sometimes it is fear that writes its perplexity which darkens the features. Sometimes it is baffled longing. Here it is desire to look into the future; again it is eagerness to learn more of God.

We are sent to be interpreters, each in his own way, and in the things which he knows. All the rich knowledge of the world has come down to us through human interpreters. All along the ages there have been men who have climbed to the mountain tops, where they saw the earliest gleams of light, while it was yet dark in the valley of life below, and have then come down and spoken to men of what they saw. There have been seers in every age, gifted to look upon the scrolls of truth and read off the words written there. The scientific knowledge we have learned to read God's words in nature. To most people nature's wonderful writings mean almost nothing, — flowers, trees, rivers, lakes, seas, mountains, the splendor of the skies, — people walk amid these divine works without awe, seeing nothing to touch their hearts or thrill their spirits. As Mrs. Browning says:

> "Earth's crammed with heaven,
> And every common bush afire with God;
> But only he who sees takes off his shoes;
> The rest sit round it, and pick blackberries."

But there have been interpreters — men with eyes which saw, with ears which heard, and they have told us something of the meaning of the wonderful things God has written in his works.

Or take the literature of the world. It is the harvest of many centuries of thought. In every age there have been men who have looked into truth with deeper, clearer vision than their fellows, and heard whispers of God's voice; then coming forth from their valleys of silence they have told the world what they heard. Take the treasures of spiritual truth which we possess; how have they come to us? Not through any scrolls brought from heaven by angels, but through human interpreters. God took Moses up into the mount and talked with him, as a man talks with his friend, revealing to him great truths about his being and character, and giving him statutes and laws for the guidance of men; then Moses became an interpreter to the world of the things which God had spoken to him. David was an interpreter for God. God drew him close to his own heart and breathed heavenly songs into his soul; then David went forth and struck his harp and sang — and the music is breathing yet through all the world. John was an interpreter for God. He lay in Christ's bosom heard the beatings of that great heart of love, and learned the secrets of friendship with his Lord; then he passed out among men and told the world what he had heard and felt and seen; and the air of this earth has been warmer ever since and more of love has been beating in human hearts. Paul was an interpreter for God. God took him away from men and revealed himself to him, opened to him the mystery of redemption as to no other man in all Christian history; and Paul wrote the letters of his which we have, which have been marvelous in their influence all these Christian centuries.

But not alone have these inspired men been God's interpreters; many others since have taken up the word of God and have found new secrets, blessed truths, precious comforts, that had lain undiscovered before, and have spoken out to men what they have found. Evermore new light is breaking from the Bible.

God gives to every life that he sends into this world some message of its own to give out to others. To one it is a new revealing of science. Kepler spoke of himself as thinking over God's thoughts, as he discovered the paths of the stars and traced out the laws of the heavens. To the poet God gives thought of beauty, revealings of the inner life, which he is to interpret to the world; and the world is richer, sweeter, and better for hearing his messages. Even to the lowliest man God whispers some secret of truth which he wants that man to impart by word or act to others. We cannot all make books, or write poems or hymns which shall bless men; but if we live near the heart of Christ there is not one of us into whose ear Christ will not speak some fragment of truth, some revealing of grace and love, or to whom he will not give some experience of comfort in sorrow, some glimpse of light in darkness, some glimmering of heaven's glory in the midst of this world's care. God forms a close personal friendship with each of his children, and tells each some special secret of love which no other ever has learned before. That now is your message — God's own peculiar word to you; and you are God's prophet to forth-tell it again to the world. Each one should speak out what God has given him to speak. If it be but a single word, it will yet bless the earth. Not to speak it will leave the world a little poorer.

Says Mozoomdar: "If the flowers should no longer be in the world, if the sun should no longer shine, how great would be our distress! If the bird no longer twittered on the budding bough of the tree, how greatly we should miss it! Everything is so closely connected with us that we cannot do without it. Everything has its corresponding fact in human nature, and every little thing has a destiny, a message. Orientals believe that each man and woman has a message, and the man or woman who accomplishes it is a true man or a true woman, but one who does not is an anomaly — one to be pitied."

We dare not hide in our heart the message that God gives us to utter to the world. Suppose that Joseph, knowing by divine teaching the meaning of Pharaoh's dreams, had remained silent, think what his silence would have cost the world. Or suppose that John, having leaned upon the Lord's breast and having learned the inner secrets of his love, had gone back to his fishing, after the ascension, and had refused or failed to be an interpreter for Christ, what would the world have lost! If one only of the million flowers that bloom in the summer days, in the fields and gardens, refused to bloom, hiding its gift of beauty, the world would be a little less lovely for the failure of the one flower. If but one of the myriad stars in the heavens should refuse to shine some night, keeping its beam locked in its own breast, the night would be a little darker. Every human life that fails to hear its message and learn its lesson, or that fails to interpret its own secret, keeping it locked in the silence of the breast, in some measure impoverishes the earth, and withholds that which would have enriched earth's life. But every life, even the lowliest, that learns its word from God and then interprets it to others, adds something, at least, to the world's sum of blessing and good. We need only to be pure in our purpose and strong in our struggle, and all life shall be purer and stronger through our faithfulness.

> "There's never a rose in all the world
> But makes some green spray sweeter;
> There's never a wind in all the sky
> But makes some bird wing fleeter;
> There's never a star but brings to heaven
> Some silver radiance tender;
> And never a rosy cloud but helps
> To crown the sunset splendor;
> No robin but may thrill some heart,
> His dawnlight gladness voicing.
> God gives us all some small sweet way,
> To set the world rejoicing.

It is our mission then to live near the heart of Christ, that we may catch the spirit of his life, and then to go forth among the people to interpret to them the things of Christ which we have learned. Then it is not our words that the world needs, so much as the sweet life that we can live. Let us get into our heart the word and spirit and love of Christ, and then interpret in our daily walk among men the beauty of Christ.

> "The dear Lord's best interpreters
> Are humble human souls;
> The gospel of a life
> Is more than books or scrolls.
>
> From scheme and creed the light goes out—
> The saintly fact survives;
> The blessed Master none can doubt
> Revealed in holy lives."

Chapter 13

Secrets of a Beautiful Life

"We are but sketches of what one day,
After the hard lines pass away,
God, the Designer, would have us to be;
Only in charcoal, rude and rough,
The mere cartoons of his greater skill."

We all want to make our lives beautiful. At least, one who has no such desire is not living worthily. We are God's children, and should live as those who have heaven's glory in their souls. We have within us immortal possibilities, and he is as one dead who does not strive to realize the beauty that is folded up in his life.

A beautiful life is one that fulfils its mission. "Every man's life is a plan of God," is a familiar saying. One who attains that for which he was made, lives beautifully, however lowly his life may be. Completeness is beauty. The meaning of the root word for 'sin' is, missing the mark. The aim is to keep God's commandments, to do God's will, to realize God's purpose. We miss the mark, and the beauty is marred. Transgression" is a like word, meaning stepping out of the path, over the boundary; that is, not walking as God directs, failing to live according to the divine plan and pattern. "Iniquity" has also a similar suggestion, — unequalness, injustice, not according to the law of right, and therefore unbeautiful.

Thus the words which describe wrong-doing all suggest marring, spoiling, the failure to fulfil the perfect design. It is as if an architect were to make a plan for a perfect building, and the builder, through ignorance of carelessness, should spoil the house, not making it like the plan. The building is not beautiful when finished, because it is not what the architect intended it to be. A life which fulfils the divine Architect's purpose, whether it be great and conspicuous, or lowly and obscure, is beautiful. We need not seek to do large things; the greatest thing for ny human life in this world is God's will for that life. That is the only true beauty.

There are some special words which may be said to hold the

secret of beauty in a life. One is "victoriousness." Many people let themselves be defeated almost habitually. It begins in childhood. The lessons are hard, and the child does not master them. It costs exertion to succeed in the games, and the boy indolently concludes that he cannot win, and does not do his best. The girl finds that she cannot play her exercises on the piano without a great deal of tiresome practice, and lets herself be defeated. It is hard to restrain temper and appetite in youth, and the young man gives up the struggle, and yields to the indulgence. Thus at the very beginning the battle is lost, and ofttimes all life afterward carries the debilitating effect. Always duty is to large, and lessons are too hard, and discipline is too severe, and passion is too strong. To its close the life is weak, never victorious, unable to cope with its environment. It is a fatal thing to form in youth the habit of permitting one's self to be defeated. Life then never can be what it might have become.

On the other hand, when the lesson of being victorious is learned in childhood, all is different. Studies are mastered; exercises are played over a hundred times, if need be, till they are played accurately; games are not indolently lost for want of exertion. Later in life, when the lessons are larger and the discipline is sorer, and the tasks require more labor, and the battles test the soul to its last particle of strength, the habit of overcoming still avails and the life is ever victorious. The thought of giving up is never entertained for a moment. The Indians say that, when a man kills a foe, the strength of the slain enemy passed into the victor's arm. In the weird fancy lies a truth. Each defeat leaves us weaker for the next battle, but each conquest makes us stronger.

Pitiable indeed is the weakness of the vanquished spirit in the face of temptation, duty, toil, or sorrow. But it is possible for us always to be overcomers. We may meet duty with a quiet confidence that shall enable us to do it well. We may be victorious in our struggles with temptation, keeping ourselves unspotted from the world. We may so relate ourselves to our conditions and our circumstances that we shall be masters, not slaves; that our very hindrances shall become helps to us, inspirers of courage and persistence.

"Stone walls do not a prison make."

Nothing makes a prison to a human life but a defeated, broken spirit. The bird in its cage that sings all the while is not a captive. God puts his children in no conditions in which he does not mean them to live sweetly and victoriously. So in any circumstances we may be "more than conquerors through him that loved us."

We may be victorious also in sorrow. If we are not, we are living below our privilege as Christians. We sin when we lie crushed, refusing to be comforted in our grief. Sorrow hurts us if we meet it with resistance and rebellion. The secret of blessing in trial lies in acquiescence. This takes out of it its bitterness and its poison, and makes it a blessing to us. One writes of sorrow;—

> "'Look thou beyond the evening sky,' she said,
> 'Beyond the changing splendors of the day;
> Accept the pain, the weariness, the dread,—
> Accept and bid me stay.'
>
> I turned and clasped her close with sudden strength;
> And slowly, sweetly, I became aware,
> Within my arms God's angel stood at length,
> White-robed and calm and fair.
>
> And now I look beyond the evening star,
> Beyond the changing splendor of the day;
> Knowing the pain he sends more precious far,
> More beautiful then they!"

The lesson of victoriousness is one of the secrets of a beautiful life. Come what may, we are not overcome. Nothing hurts us; all things help us. The common antagonisms of life climb step by step, nearer God and nearer heaven. Christ was victorious in his life, and so may we be if we put our feet over in the prints of his shoes.

Another of the secrets of a beautiful life is found in the word "serving." Our Lord gave us the full truth when he said of his own mission, that he came, "not to be ministered unto, but to minister." When we understand the meaning of this word, and then relate ourselves to all others about us in accordance with this standard, we begin to be a blessing to every one. Our thought then ever is, not what we can get of pleasure, of help, of profit, of comfort, of good in any form, from others, but what we can give to them. True loving is not receiving, but giving. The Christlike desire toward our friends is not that we may get something from them, that they may be of use to us, but that in some way we may be a blessing to them, may do them good. This feeling will restrain us from ever harming another in any way. It will keep us from offering temptation to another. It will make us watchful of our influence over others, lest in some way we cast a hurtful instead of a healing shadow upon them. It will also temper our demands of others, since we are seeking, not to be ministered unto, but to minister. It will turn the whole thought of our life from the mere seeking of happiness to the doing of good to others, the giving of happiness.

> "Life were not worth the living,
> If no one were the better
> For having met thee on the way,
> And know the sunshine of thy stay.
> Give as thy God is giving;
> To no one be a debtor!
> So hearts shall faster beat for thee,
> And faces beam thy light to see."

Some people have a great deal of trouble looking after their rights, seeing that no one wrongs them, that they always get proper honor and attention from others, and that no injustice is ever done to them. We hear echoes of this human striving breaking out from the heart of certain great and splendid pageants, where the grand participants contend for precedence in rank, for degree of nobility, at the table or in the procession. We find it in much lowlier places, in society, and in the common walks, in the clamor for the highest distinction or for honor among men. We are spared all such trouble if we have this law of serving deep in our hearts. Our only care then is that we do not ourselves wrong others, even if they have treated us unjustly or unkindly.

The highest rank with Christ is the fullest, truest serving. When we have learned this lesson, we are prepared to be a blessing to every life that touches ours, even for a moment, in passing; as when two ships meet, speak each other, and move each on its own way. Our entire attitude toward others is changed; we look upon every human being as one who possibly needs something we have to give, one to whom we have errand of love, one whom we must wish God-speed, one for whom we must at least breathe a whispered prayer.

This is the heart of Christlikeness as interpreted in practical living. It is the real secret of happiness too; for it is more blessed to give than to receive — not more pleasant to nature, but more blessed. We vex ourselves then no longer about the lack of gratitude in others, about the exact of reciprocal attention or favor, about whose turn it is to call, or write, or whose place it is to take the first step toward reconciliation. Love keeps no debit and credit accounts, and seeks only to be always first in serving.

Another secret of sweet and happy Christian life is in learning to live by the day. It is the long stretches that tire us. We cannot carry this load until we are threescore and ten. We cannot fight this battle continually for half a century. But really there are no long stretches. Life does not come to us in lifetimes; it comes only a day at a time. Even to-morrow is never ours till it becomes to-day, and we have nothing whatever to do with it, but to pass down to it a fair and good inheritance in to-day's work well done and to-day's life well lived.

It is a blessed secret, this of living by the day. Any one can carry his burden, however heavy, till nightfall. Any one can do his work, however hard, for one day. Any one can live sweetly, quietly, patiently, lovingly, and purely till the sun goes down. And this is all that life really ever means to us, — just one little day. "Do to-day's duty, fight to-day's temptation, and do not weaken and distract yourself by looking forward to things you cannot see, and could not understand if you saw them." God gives us nights to shut down the curtain of darkness on our little days. We cannot see beyond, and we ought not to try to see beyond. Short horizons make life easier, and give us one of the blessed secrets of brave, true, holy living.

These are some of the secrets of a beautiful life. We ought not to be content to live otherwise than beautifully. We can live our life only once. We cannot go over it again to correct its mistakes or amend its faults. We ought therefore to live it well. And to do this we must begin at the beginning, and make every day radiant as it passes. Lost days must always remain blanks in the records, and stained days must carry their stains. Beautiful days make beautiful years, and beautiful years make a beautiful life at its close.

Chapter 14

Helping by Prayer

"Yes, pray for whom thou lovest; if uncounted wealth were thine—
the treasures of the boundless deep, the riches of the mine—
Thou couldst not to thy cherished friends a gift so dear impart,
As the earnest benediction of a deeply prayerful heart."

FRIENDSHIP which does not pray lacks a most sacred element.
It leaves God out, and that is leaving out friendship's best possibilities of blessing. Earth's sweetest joy needs heaven to make it
complete. Wisely has it been written, "Pray for whom thou lovest;
thou wilt never have any comfort of his friendship for whom thou
dost not pray." Certain it is, at least, that truest, deepest, realest
comfort cannot come to us from a friend whose name we do not
speak to God in love's pleading. The holiest experience of friendship is in communion with God. Only to God can the heart's most
sacred longings for a friend be uttered.

"Yes, pray for whom thou lovest; thou mayest vainly, idly seek
The fervid thoughts of tenderness by feeble words to speak.
Go, kneel before thy Father's throne, and meekly, humbly there
Ask blessing for the loved one in the silent hour of Prayer.
And should thy flowery path of life become a path of pain,
The friendship formed in bonds like these thy spirit shall sustain;
Years may not chill, nor change invade, nor poverty impair
The love that grew and flourished at the holy time of prayer."

God has put it in our power to help each other in many ways, —
sometimes by deeds that lift away burdens, sometimes by words
that inspire courage and strength, sometimes by sympathy that
halves sorrow; but there is no other way in which we can serve our
friends so wisely, so effectively, so divinely, as by intercession for
them. Our hands are clumsy and unskillful, and ofttimes hurt the
life we would heal with our touch, or strengthen and uphold with
our strength; but in prayer we can reach our friend through God,
and God's hand is infinitely gentle, and never hurts a life. We lack

wisdom, and ofttimes the help we give is untimely or inwise. We would lift away burdens that God wants our friend to carry. We would make the way easy for him when God has made it hard for his own good, for the development of his powers. We would save our friend from hardship or self-denial, or hold him back from perilous duty or exhausting service, when these are the very paths in which God would lead him — the paths to honor, to larger usefulness, to nobler life. Ofttimes our love is shortsighted. We think we are helping our friend, when really we are hindering him in the things that most deeply concern his life. But we can pray and ask God to help him, not in our way but in his own way, and God's help is never unwise nor intimely. He never lifts away a load which our friend would be the better for carrying. He never does things for him which he would better be left to do for himself, nor spares him hardness or suffering which will make him more a man.

There are times, too, when we can help with our love in no other way but by prayer. The friend is beyond our reach, or his experiences of need are such that we can do nothing for him. Human capacity for helpfulness is very small. We can give a piece of bread when one is hungry, or a cup of cold water when one is thirsty, or raiment when one is naked, or medicine when one is sick. But in the deeper needs of life we can do nothing. Our words are only mockeries. Yet we can pray, and God can send his own help to the heart in any experience.

Thus we get hints of the truth that the noblest, divinest way of helping our friends is by prayer. It follows, therefore, that we sin against them when we do not help them in this best and truest of all ways — by praying for them. The parent who does not pray for a child, whatever else he may do for him, sins against the child. Whoever fails to pray for one he loves fails in the most sacred duty of love, because he withholds love's best help. "A prayerlesss love may be tender, and may speak murmuring words of sweetest sound; but it lacks the deepest expression and the noblest music of speech. We never help our dear ones so well as when we pray for them."

It is pleasant to think that this best of all service for others we can render even when unable to do any active work on their behalf. A "shut in" who can run no errands and lift no burdens and speak no words of cheer to busy toilers and sore strugglers in the great world, can yet pray for them, and God will send truest help. Said a good man, when laid aside from active service: "One thought has assumed a new reality in my mind of late, as an offshoot of my useless life. When a man can do nothing else, he can add his little rill to the great river of intercessory prayer which is always rolling up to the throne of God. The river is made up of such rills, as the ocean is of drops. A praying man can never be a useless man."

Again the same writer says: "You do not know how my soul longs to get into closer friendship with Christ, and to pray — which is about the only mode of usefulness left to me — as he prayed. To touch the springs of the universe as he touched them! One can almost feel the electric thrill of it." We cannot tell what intercessory prayer does for the world — for our own lives.

> "More things are wrought by prayer
> than this world dreams of."

It is well, also, that we think carefully of the things we ask for our friends. There is the same danger that exists in prayers for ourselves — that we press only our will for them, and request for them only things of an earthly kind. There is a good model for all intercession in the way Epaphras prayed for his friends in Colosse: "Always laboring fervently for you in prayers, that ye may stand perfect and complete in all the will of God." It is not merely health and prosperity and success in life that we are to ask for those we love, but that God's will may be done in them, and that they may fulfil his plan and purpose for them.

The mother's prayer for her children should not be, first, that they may win worldly honor, but that they may be complete in all God's will, may be what God made them to be. The best place they can reach in this world is that for which God designed them when he gave them their being.

Ofttimes we are led to pray for our friends when they are in some trouble. For example, one we love is sick. We are touched with sympathy, and go to God with our heart's burden. What shall our prayer be? That our friend may recover? Yes, that is love's right and natural prayer, and we may ask this very earnestly. Jesus prayed three times that his own cup of sorrow might pass. But that must not be all of our prayer. It would be very sad if our friend were to get well, and were not to take some blessing out of his sick-room with him when he leaves it. Therefore we are to pray that he may be enriched in spiritual experience; that he may be made a better man through his illness; that he may be brought into close relation with Christ; that his life may be purified; that he may be made more thoughtful, gentle, unselfish, unworldly, more like Christ; in a word, that he may be made perfect and complete in all the will of God.

It may become needful to qualify the prayer that our friend shall recover. It may be God's will that he should now go home. We may still give full vent to love's yearning that he shall get well; but at the close of our intense supplication we must submit it all to God's wisdom in the refrain, "Nevertheless, not as I will, but as thou wilt." If love be true, it is always the very best thing that we ask for our dear ones when we pray for them; and the best — God's best — for them may be, not longer life in this world, but heaven, the crowning of their life in immortal glory and blessedness.

Or our friend may be in some trouble. He may be staggering under a heavy load, and it may seem to us that the best blessing which could come to him would be the lifting away of the load. But, as we begin to pray, we remember that the truest and most loving prayer for him must be that he shall stand perfect and complete in all God's will. Possibly his load is part of God's will to bring out the best that is in him.

In all our praying for our friends we are to think first of their higher, spiritual good. We are to seek for them above all things that they may grow into all the beauty of perfect Christian character. It is a poor, superficial friendship which desires chiefly our friend's present ease and mere earthly good. It is asking for him a stone instead of bread, a scorpion instead of an egg, or a serpent instead of a fish. Those who seek for their friends only earthly things, are choosing for them only the husks, and omitting to choose for them the golden grain which would feed their immortal nature. We sin against our loved ones when we seek for them merely the things or own frail, shortsighted judgment may desire for them. Love is true only when it rises into heavenly heights, and craves, for those that are dear, the things of God's own blessed perfect will. This is not always easy. It is hard for us to say, "They will be done," when it means that or loved one must endure sore pain, or walk in deep shadows, or be humbled under God's mighty hand.

But, whether for our friends or for ourselves, we dare not in prayers press our own wishes against God's. "Even though it be a cross that raiseth" must be our cry for our dearest as well as for ourselves. The standard of pleading must be the same. And some day we shall see and know that our love was truest when it asked even pain and loss for one who was dear, because it was God's will.

"I sometimes think God's heart must ache,
Listening to all the sad, complaining cries,
That from our weak, impatient souls arise,
Because we do not see that for our sake
He answers not, or answers otherwise
Than seems the best to our tear-blinded eyes.
This is love's hardest task, to do hard things
For love's own sake, then bear the murmurings
Of ignorance, too dull to judge aright
The love that rises to this wond'rous height
He knows we have not yet attained; and so
He wearies not, but bears complaint and moan,
And shields each willing heart against his own,
Knowing that some glad day we too shall know."

Chapter 15

The Cost of Praying

"Say, what is prayer, when it is prayer indeed?
The mighty utterance of a mighty need.
The man is praying who doth press with might
Out of his darkness into God's own light."

It seems easy to pray. It is only speaking a few simple words in our Father's ear. We are not accustomed to think of praying as something hard. Yet sometimes it is only at sore cost that we can pray. Many of the things we ask for can come to us only through struggle and tears.

The basis of all praying is the submission of the whole life to the will of God. We cannot pray at all unless we make this full surrender. There is a story of a young naval officer who was taken prisoner. Brought into the presence of the commandant of the victorious squadron, he reached out his hand to him, his sword yet hanging by his side. "Your sword first," said his captor. No greeting or salutation could be accepted until surrender was complete. Nor can we approach God in acceptable prayer until we have altogether submitted our will to his. All our prayers must be based upon "Thy will, not mine, be done." It costs much to make this surrender. It means a giving up of our own will and our own way. When it is sincere and real, every kneeling at Christ's feet is a laying of one's self upon the altar anew in entire devotion. We can keep nothing back and pray truly. A sin cherished makes words of prayer of no avail. A plan, a wish, a desire, willfully urged, not submitted to God's perfect will, pressed rebelliously, shut the ear of God to our praying. To pray means always the sacrifice of the will.

Is it, then, never hard to pray? Does it cost nothing? Are there no struggles with self, no giving up of desires dear as life, no dropping of cherished things out of the hand, no crushing of tender human affections, in the quiet "Thy will be done" of our prayers? It was something you wanted, but you were not sure God wanted you to have it. You prayed earnestly for it, but you said, "They will, not mine, be done." The gift did not come, but your desire became less and less intense as you prayed and waited. At least, when it became evident that it was not God's will to grant your wish, there was no bitterness no lingering struggle, only peace and a song. But did the submission cost you nothing?

Or it was a sorrow against which you pleaded. A loved one was stricken. With all your heart you prayed that your friend might recover. Yet, as you prayed, you were led by gentle constraint to lay the burden of your desire in submission at God's feet. Slowly, as the days and nights of watching went by, and the illness grew worse instead of better, and when it became more and more certain that your dear one would be taken from you, there came into your heart a new, strange sense of God's love, and you were calm and quiet. Then, when the sorrow came, there was no rebellion, no bitterness, but only sweet trust. All this wondrous change your praying had wrought in you. It had not changed God's way, bringing it down to yours, but it had lifted you up into accord with God's will. Did it cost you nothing?

This is the inner history of every praying life. We ask for things we desire, things which we think would make us happier. Yet these things which we think would be bread to our hearts would really prove a stone if we had them. Our Father will never give his child a stone for bread, and hence the story of much of our praying is a story of unanswered prayers — unanswered in a sense. The things we want must be given up. Self must die. Desire must yield. Faith must grow. Our wills must blend with God's. Our restlessness must nestle in his rest. Our struggle must become quiet in his peace. We must be lifted up nearer to God. Such struggle costs — costs anguish and tears, but it brings us rich good. No doubt many of our best blessings come through God's withholdings. Ofttimes it is more blessed to learn to do without things than it would be to get them. The prayer is not really unanswered in such cases. The things we asked for would not have been a blessing; but the very longing, though it was not satisfied, did us good, made us stronger, lifted us up into better life, while the lesson of submission learned through struggle and pain was rich in its discipline. It is in such experiences that we grow upward toward God. Writes Sarah K. Bolton:—

> "Life is full of broken measures,
> Objects unattained:
> Sorrows intertwined with pleasures,

Losses of our costliest treasures,
Ere the heights be gained.

Every soul has aspiration
Still unsatisfied:
Memories that wake vibration
Of the heart in quick pulsation,
At the gifts denied.

We are better for the longing,
Stronger for the pain:
Souls at ease are nature wronging;—
Through the harrowed soul come thronging
Seeds, in sun and rain!

Broken measures, fine completeness
In the perfect whole:
Life is but a day in fleetness
Richer in all strength and sweetness
Grows the striving soul."

But such lessons are not easily learned. Such discipline is not easily gotten. It always costs to pray the soul in calmness and peace. The struggle grows less and less as the praying goes on; the pleadings are less intense; at last they sob themselves into silence, and the lips speak with love and trust the word of submission. But is has been at sore cost that this result has been gained. It was the dying of self that was going on. Such praying costs.

There is another phase of the cost of praying. We ask for more holiness. We know that this is God's will for us, and yet it may require a long time of struggle to bring our lives into true accord with our own desire. We pray to be made more humble, but it is probable that our longing can be answered only through many buffetings and defeats. We ask for patience, but the very word tells of suffering to be endured, and the quality of patience is one that can be gotten only through trail. We ask for more of Christ in our heart, and God is very willing to grant us this request. But perhaps our heart is so preoccupied that room for more of Christ can be made only by the casting out of many other things. Here is where the cost is experienced. The old nature in us will not yield to the new without a protest, nor until vanquished and put under foot.

It is never easy to grow better. You pray for a gentle temper. Does it come quietly and softly in answer to your prayer, as the dove came down out of the heavens to abide on Christ at his baptism? This certainly is not the usual history of the evolution of a sweet temper. It is a story rather of sore and long discipline, in which a turbulent and uncontrolled spirit is, by a slow process, tamed and trained into self-control, ofttimes only through long and sore struggle and many failures. When a man with an ungoverned temper begins to pray sincerely and earnestly that he may learn to rule his own spirit and to grow into lovingness of disposition, he does not know what it will cost him to have his prayer answered. It is the same with all sincere requests for Christlikeness. We have the impression that a few petitions breathed up to God, asking him to make us pure, loving, and gentle, will bring the answer in some mysterious way, working the change in us without any effort or struggle of our own. But it is not thus that such prayers are answered.

John Newton, in one of his hymns, tells the story of such a prayer. He asked the Lord that he might grow in faith, and love, and every grace. He hoped that in some favored hour the request would be at once answered, and his sins subdued by love's restraining power. Instead of this, however, he was made to feel the hidden evils of his heart, and his soul was assaulted by the angry powers of darkness.

> "'Lord, why is this?' I trembling cried;
> 'Wilt thou pursue thy worm to death?'
> ''Tis in this way,' the Lord replied,
> "I answer prayer for grace and faith;
>
> These inward trails I employ
> From self and pride to set thee free;
> And break thy schemes of earthly joy,
> That thou mayest seek thine all in me.'"

They know not what they ask who begin to pray sincerely and deeply, "Nearer, my God to thee." It may indeed require a cross to lift us higher and nearer. But no price is too great to pay to become conquerors over self, and to grow into holiness and beauty of life.

Another example of the cost of praying is found in prayers for others. Sometimes it is easy enough to pray for our friends, and seems to involve nothing on our part. But we do not pray long for others with true earnestness and with the importunity of love, before we find that we have something to do to make our praying avail. A parent's pleading for a child draws the parent's whole soul with it. We pray for the heathen; and, unless we are heartlessly insincere, we must take a corresponding interest in movements to save the heathen. We pray for the sick, the poor, the needy; and if we mean it at all, our love will not stop at praying. A city missionary implored God to send his angel to care for two orphan children whom he had found in a cold, fireless hovel, starving and naked beside the dead body of their mother. Instantly a voice spoke to him in his conscience, "Thou art mine angel; for this very purpose did I send thee here." His praying for these children proved a costly act. You would better not begin pleading for one of God's little ones in need or trouble, telling God of your interest in the suffering one, if you want your praying to cost you nothing. Almost surely God will ask you to care for the suffering one for him.

We are to pray for our enemies, for those who despitefully use us. That is not easy. It costs no struggle when we go home in the evening and kneel down before God in our closet, to recall all who have been gentle and kind to us, and to pray for them. Anybody can do that. But we are to recall also and especially those who have been unkind to us, who have spoken evil of us, of have injured us in some way, and are to pray for these. And praying for them involves forgiveness in every case. We cannot keep the resentment, the angry feeling, the grudge, after truly praying for those who have done us hurt. At the altar of intercessory prayer all anger, passion, and bitterness die. Praying for others sweeps out of our heart everything but love. Thus it proves very costly, but the blessing it brings is very rich.

These are illustrations of the cost of praying. Every true spiritual longing is a reaching up out of self into a better, truer, nobler life. Praying is always a climbing upward toward God. We can thus climb only at the cost of struggle and self-denial, the crucifixion of the old nature. David said he would not offer to God that which had cost him nothing. In prayer the same test can be applied. Pleadings that cost nothing have no answer. Prayers that cost the most bring down the richest blessings.

Chapter 16

Making Friendship Hard

"Mine be the love that in itself can find
Seed of white thoughts, the lilies of the mind,
Seed of that glad surrender of the will
Which finds in service self's true purpose still."

The secret of being a friend lives in the power to give and do and serve without thought of return. It is not easy. Wanting to have a friend is altogether different from wanting to be a friend. The former is a mere natural human craving; the latter is the life of Christ in the soul. Christ craved friendship, but he longed always to be a friend. Every life that came before him he desired to help and bless in some way. He never tired of the faults and imperfections of his disciples; he was not seeking mere pleasure for himself in them, but was striving to do them good. Hence he never grew tired of them. His interest in them was like that of a kindly physician in his patient.

Wherever the spirit of Christ is in a human heart this same desire is found. True friendship is unwearied in doing good, in serving and helping others. Yet it is only right that the other side of being a friend should have attention. We must not put the love and unselfishness of our friends to too sore a testing.

There are some people who make it very hard for others to be their friends. They put friendship to unreasonable tests. They make demands upon it to which only the largest patience and the most generous charity will submit.

There are some persons who complain that they have no friends, and ofttimes the complaint may be almost true. There are none with whom they have close personal friendship. They have no friend who is ready to share in all their life, rejoicing with them in their joys, and bearing beside them and with them their load of care, sorrow, or anxiety. They seem without real companionship, although all about them throng other lives with the very things of love for which their hearts are crying out.

These unfriended ones think the fault is with the other people, whom they regard as cold, uncongenial, selfish. But really the fault is with themselves. They make it all but impossible for anyone to be their close personal friend. Nothing less holy and less divine than mother-love can endure the exactions and demands they put upon those who would be glad, if they could, to stand in the relation of friends to them.

A close friendship can be formed and can continue to exist only where there is mutal unselfishness. It cannot all be on one side. We cannot expect our friend to give all while we give nothing. We cannot ask that he be generous, patient, confiding, self-denying, and thoughtful toward us, while we in our bearing toward him lack all these qualities. Christ bears with us in all our sad faultiness, is patient toward all our weakness, infirmity, and sin; and is our faithful, unfailing friend, though we give him but little love, and that little mingled with doubts, complainings, murmurings, and ingratitude. Many of us make it hard for Christ to be our friend; yet he loves unto the end, unto the uttermost. Elisabeth Stuart Phelps writes:—

> "Thine the bearing and forbearing
> Through the patient years;
> Thine the loving, and the moving
> Plea of sacred tears.
> Thine the caring and the wearing
> Of my pain for me;
> Thine the sharing and the bearing
> Of my sin of thee.
> Mine the leaving and the grieving
> Of thy mournful eyes;
> Mine the fretting and forgetting
> Of our blood-bound ties.
> Mine the plaining and complaining,
> And complaining still;
> Mine the fearing and the wearying
> Of thy tender will.
> Mine the wrecking, thine the building,
> Of our happiness —
> My only Saviour, help me make
> The dreadful difference less."

The mothers come next to Christ in their friendship, — patient, unwearying, without return. Many children make it very hard even for their mother to be their friend, putting her love to very sore tests. Yet she too loves on in the face of all ingratitude, unkindness, unworthiness.

But there are few others who will be such friends to us as Christ and our mothers, who will be so patient with us, who will love us and love on when we do not take our just share of the friendship, or when we give only hurt or ingratitude in return for love and tenderness. There are few outside our own family who will take the trouble to maintain close relations with us, when we make it as hard as we can for them to do so. There may be one or two persons among those who know us, who have love disinterested enough to cling to us in spite of all our wounding of their affection, and all the needless burden we put upon their faithfulness. But such friends are rare, and the man is fortunate who has even one who will be such a friend to him while he puts the friendship to such unreasonable proof.

There are many ways in which friendship is made hard. One way is by doubting and by questioning. There are those who demand repeated assertion and assurance in word, every time they meet their friend, that he is still their friend. If he fails to put his abiding, loyal interest into some fervent, oft-repeated formula of constancy, they begin to wonder if he has not changed in his feeling toward them, and perhaps tell him of their anxiety. A little thought will show any one how hard friendship is made by such a course as this. This spirit indicates want of full trust, and nothing more effectually stunts and deadens the heart's gentle affections then being doubted. It indicates also sentimentality, which is very unwholesome.

Such demand for reiterated avowal may be pardoned in very young lovers who have not yet attained to manly or womanly strength. But in the relations of common friendship it should never be made. The moment a true-hearted man, eager to be helpful to another, finds the sentimental spirit creeping in, he is embarrassed in his effort to do a friend's part; and, if he is not a man of large patience and unwearying kindness, he will find his helpfulness greatly hindered. Many an earnest desire to be a friend is rendered altogether unavailing by such a spirit. In any case, friendship is made hard for a man, however loyal and unselfish he may be.

Another way in which friendship is made hard is by an exacting spirit. There are those who seem to think of a friend only as one who should help them. They value him in proportion to the measure of his usefulness to them. Hence they expect him to show them favors at every point, and to do many things for them. They do not seem to have any conception of the lofty truth that the heart of friendship is not the desire to receive, but the desire to give. We cannot claim to be served by him. We are only declaring our unmitigated selfishness when we act on this principle.

Yet there are those who would exact all and give nothing. Their friend may show them kindnesses in unbroken continuity for years, doing perhaps ofttimes important things for them; but the moment he declines or omits to grant some new favor which they have sought, all past acts are instantly forgotten.

There are a few generous people who do not repeatedly have just this experience. Of course no return in favors is desired by a true friend. There are many cases indeed in which, in one sense, the helpfulness of the friendship must necessarily be all on one side. It may be so when one is an invalid, unable to do anything, compelled to be a burden continually upon a friend. But in such a case there is a return possible which is a thousand times better than if it could be made in kind — a return of gratitude, of affection, of trust. Such a requital makes friendship easy, though the calls upon it for service may be constant and very heavy. But the spirit here referred to makes it very hard for a friend to go on carrying the load year after year. Demands upon love do not help in the nourishing of love. He who would compel our service, especially he who would enforce demands for manifestations of affection, puts his friend to a very sore test. One may be ready to give and serve and suffer for another, even to the uttermost; but one does not like to do this under compulsion, in order to meet exacting demands.

Another example is that in which one claims a friend exclusively for one's own. There are such people. They want their friend to show interest in no other, to do kindness to no other. This also might be excused in a certain kind of very sentimental young lovers, but it is not confined to such. It exists in many cases toward others of the same sex, nor is it confined to the very young. Persons have been known to demand that the one who is their friend shall be theirs so exclusively as scarcely to treat others respectfully. Any pleasant courtesy to another has been taken as a personal slight and hurt to the chosen "friend."

Unless both persons are alike weak and sentimental, such a spirit cannot but make friendship hard. No man or woman who has the true conception of life is willing to be bound in such chains.

We cannot fufil our mission in God's great world of human beings by permitting ourselves to be tied up in this sentimental way to any one person. No worthy friendship ever makes such demands. Love knows no such limitations; only jealousy can inspire such narrowness, and jealousy is always ignoble and dishonoring. A noble wife and husband, bound in one, in the most sacred of ties, make no such weak and selfish demand upon each other, each desires the other, while loyal and true in the closer relation, to be the largest possible blessing to all the world, knowing that their mutual love is not made less, but richer, by the exercise of unselfishness toward all who need help.

The same spirit should be manifested in all friendship, and will be manifested just so far as they are noble and exalted in character, and are set free from norrowness and jealousy. A man need be no less my friend, no less true, no less helpful to me, because he is the friend of hundreds more who turn to him with their cravings and needs, and find strength and inspiration in him. The heart grows rich in loving, and my friend becomes more to me through being the friend of others. But if I demand that he shall be my friend only, I make it very hard for him to be my friend at all.

Only a few suggestions have been given of the way in which many people make it hard for others to be their friends. Not only do they make it hard for their friends to continue their faithfulness and helpfulness to them, but they rob themselves of the full, rich blessings which they might receive, and lessen the value to them of the friendship which they would make of yet greater value. We can get the most and the best from our friends by being large-hearted and trustful ourselves, by putting no trammels on them, by making no demands or exactions, by seeking to be worthy of whatever they may wish to do for us, by accepting what their love prompts in our behalf, proving our gratitude by a friendship as sincere, as hearty, as disinterested, and as helpful as it is in our power to give. Thus shall we make it easy for others to be our friends, and shall never have occasion to say that nobody cares for us.

In what has been said, it is not intended to teach that in our friendships we should be impatient and easily wearied with the faults and imperfections of those whom we seek to help. We should not be easily offended or driven away. On the other hand, we should be as nearly perfect as possible in our patience and endurance. We should be Christlike, and Christ loves unto the uttermost. His love is not worn out by our faultiness, our dullness, nor even by our sinning. We cannot be full, rich blessings in the world unless we have in us, in large measure, the love that seeketh not its own, is not provoked, beareth all things, endureth all things, and never faileth. The capacity for being a blessing to others is a capacity for loving; and the capacity for loving is a capacity for self-denial, for long-suffering, for the giving of its own life without thought of return.

To many it does not seem worth while to give labor and thought and time and strength and patience and comfort at such cost, to help along through life the weak, the broken, the sinning, ofttimes the unreasonable, the ungrateful. But it was thus that Christ lived, and there is no other standard of living that will reach up to the divine ideal. Besides, it is such losing of self that is the only real saving of a life.

Chapter 17

Give Ye Them to Eat

"My life is not my own, but Christ's, who gave it,
And he bestows it upon all the race;
I lose it for his sake, and thus I save it;
I hold it close, but only to expend it;
Accept it, Lord, for others, through thy grace!"

We begin to live only when we begin to love, and we begin to love only when self dies and we live to bless others. We forget too often that we are the body of Christ in this world. The things he would do for men we must do. His pity for the lost must throb in our human hearts. His comfort for earth's sorrow must be spoken by human lips. He is the bread of life which alone can feed men's hunger, but it must pass through our hands. We must be the revealers of Christ to others. The love must flow to them through us. We are the branches, and from our little lives must drop the fruits which shall meet men's cravings.

The importance of this human part is well illustrated in our Lord's miracle of the feeding of the five thousand. When the need of the people was spoken of, the disciples proposed to send them away to buy bread for themselves. Jesus replied, "They have no need to go away; give ye them to eat." No wonder the disciples were startled by such a command, when they realized the smallness of their own resources. Yet a little later they did give the multitudes to eat from their own small stores, and had abundance left for themselves.

The miracle is for our instruction. All about us are those who have many and sore need. We pity them. We turn to Christ with our pity, and pray him to send some one to feed and bless those who are in such need. But as we listen we hear him say, "Give ye them to eat!" Then we say, "Why, Master, we have nothing to give to these hungry multitudes. We cannot comfort these sorrows. We cannot guide these tottering, stumbling feet. We cannot give strength to these fainting hearts. We cannot meet these intense cravings for sympathy, for love, for life. We cannot feed these hungers. We have only our five barley loaves, and here are thousands." But our Lord's quiet answer still is, "Give ye them to eat."

Christ always used the human so far as the human would reach. He never wrought an unnecessary miracle. If the work could be done without the putting forth of supernatural energy, it was so wrought. And when miracles were performed, all that human ability could do in the process was left to human ability. There was never any waste of miracle. Then it is a common law in the kingdom of God that, whenever possible, divine gifts are passed to men through other men. God sends many of his gifts to the world through human hands and hearts. The word of God was spoken in olden times through human lips. When God came to reveal his love and mercy in a life, the people looked up and saw a face like their own faces. The real worker in the world to-day is the Holy Spirit. His is the power that regenerates, sanctifies, and comforts. But no eye sees him. He works invisibly, silently. What we see all the time is a human face and a human hand. We hear the Spirit's voice in the accents of lips like our own. The gospel is the be told to every creature; but those who have learned it themselves, and have been saved by it, must be the bearers of the good news. The command still and always is, "Give ye them to eat."

This puts upon us who know the love and grace of Christ a great responsibility. These who are in need or in sorrow about us must be blessed through us. The responsibility for helping, comforting, lifting up, these weak, sad or fallen ones, is with us. Yet we seem to have nothing with which to answer their cravings. We have only five barley loaves, and what are they among so many?

We may get further instruction concerning the manner of blessing the world with our meager resources, from the way the disciples fed these thousands. First, they brought their barley loaves to Christ. If they had begun feeding the people with what they had, without bringing it to the Master, it could have fed only a few. We also must bring our paltry resources to Christ, and put them into his hands. This is always the first thing in doing good. Without Christ's blessing, even the largest resources of abilities will avail nothing. Christ can do nothing with us until we have really given ourselves into his hands. But when we have done this, no one on earth can tell the measure of good that may be wrought even by the smallest abilities.

Then follows Christ's blessing on the loaves. His blessing maketh rich. We ought to pray continually that Christ's touch may be upon us, and that what we have may first lie in his hands, before it is given out to become food to others. There seems to be a significance, too, in the fact that Christ broke the loaves as he blessed them, before he gave them into the hands of the disciples. Often he must break us and our gifts before he can make us bread for others. Very beautifully do Dr. S. W. Duffield's lines illustrate this:—

> "They tell me I must bruise
> The rose's leaf
> Ere I can keep and use
> Its fragrance brief.
>
> They tell me I must break
> The skylark's heart
> Ere her cage song will make
> The silence start.
>
> They tell me love must bleed,
> And friendship weep,
> Ere in my deepest need
> I touch that deep.
>
> Must it be always so
> With precious things?
> Must they be bruised, and go
> With beaten wings?
>
> Ah, yes! By crushing days,
> By caging nights, by scar
> Of thorns and stony ways,
> These blessings are!"

Many of us cannot be used to become food for the world's hunger until we are broken in Christ's hands. "Bread corn is bruised." Christ's blessing ofttimes means sorrow, but even sorrow is not too great a price to pay for the privilege of touching other lives with benediction. The sweetest things in this world to-day have come to us through tears and pain. We need never be afraid to make sacrifices in doing good. It is the things that cost, that yield blessing. The ashes of our joys ofttimes nourish joys for other.

> "Some sweet or tender thing may grow
> To stronger life because of thee;
> Content to play an humble part,

> Give of the ashes of thy heart,
> And haply God, whose dear decrees
> Taketh from those to give to these,
> Who draws the snowdrop from the snows,
> May from these ashes feed a rose."

The last thing in this story of the feeding of the people was the passing of the broken loaves through the hands of the disciples to the people. Jesus did not distribute them himself. He gives our consecrated gifts back to us, that we may dispense them. He would teach us, for one thing, that we can be our own best almoners. Our money loses sadly in power to do good if we must pass it through a society instead of taking it ourselves to those who need it. If possible, we would better always give it with our own hands, and let our love go with it, in expressions that will be bread for the hunger of those whom we would serve.

"The gift without the giver is bare."

It is a great responsibility which this truth puts upon Christian people. The bread can reach the hungry only through the hands of the disciples. "Give ye them to eat" is still the word. The perishing world can get the blessings of the gospel of Christ only through us. Here stands the Master with the consecrated bread in his hands, enough for all. Yonder is the multitude, with countless needs and hungers. But between Christ and the people is the human ministry. "He gave the loaves to the disciples, and the disciples, to the multitude." Suppose the disciples had eaten of the bread themselves, and, when satisfied, had still remained sitting there, enjoying their blessing, but carrying it no farther; what would have been the result? The people would have gone hungry, although there had been ample provision made for them by the Master. The guilt would have been on the heads of the disciples.

But we are now Christ's disciples. All about us are hungry people. Christ has bread to give them — enough to satisfy all their hungers. But it must pass to them through our hands. What if the bread stop with us? What if we take it — this sacred bread, Christ's own body broken for us — and eat it with relish, and sit down and think not of those just beyond us who are hungering for comfort, for help, for love, for life? This bread is not given to us for ourselves alone, — Christ gives no blessing in that way; it is given for ourselves, and then to be passed on by us to others. Says Amiel, "It is better to be lost then to be saved all alone." And Susan

Coolidge writes, using Amiel's word as a motto:-

> "To lie by the river of life and see it run to waste,
> To eat of the tree of heaven while the nations go unfed,
>
> To taste the full salvation — the only one to taste —
> To live while the rest are lost — oh, better by far be dead!
>
> For to share is the bliss of heaven, as it is the joy of earth;
> And the unshared bread lacks savor, and the wine unshared lacks zest:
>
> And the joy of the soul redeemed would be little, little worth,
> If, content with its own security, it could forget the rest."

So it is that we stand between Christ and a needy, hungry world. So it is that the bidding ever comes to us, "Give ye them to eat." Let us be faithful. It would be a bitter thing, indeed, if any should perish because we did not carry to them the bread which the Master gives us for them.

Chapter 18

On Judging Others

"Don't look for the flaws as you go through life;
And even when you find them,
It is wise and kind to be somewhat blind,
And look for the virtue behind them.
For the cloudiest night has a hint of the light
Somewhere in its shadows hiding;
It is better, by far, to look for a star
Than the spots on the sun abiding."

It is better to have eyes for beauty than for blemish. It is better to be able to see the roses than the thorns. It is better to have learned to look for things to commend in others than for things to condemn. Of course other people have faults, and we are not blind. But then we have faults of our own, and this should make us charitable.

We have a divine teaching on the subject. Our Lord said, "Judge not, that ye be not judged." We need to understand just what the words mean. We cannot help judging others. We ought to be able to read character, and to know whether men are good or bad. As we watch men's acts we cannot help forming opinions about them. The holier we grow and the more like Christ, the keener will be our moral judgments. We are not bidden to shut our eyes and to be blind to people's faults and sins.

What, then, do our Lord's words mean? It is uncharitable judgment against which he warns us. We are not to look for the evil things in others. We are not to see others through the warped glasses of prejudice and unkindly feeling. We are not to arrogate to ourselves the function of judging, as if men were answerable to us. We are to avoid a critical or censorious spirit. Nothing is said against speaking of the good in those we see and know; it is uncharitable judging and speaking that are condemned.

One reason why this is wrong is that it is putting one's self in God's place. He is the one Judging with whom every human soul has to do. Judgment is not ours, but God's. "One only is the lawgiver and the judge, even he who is able to save and to destroy; but who art thou that judgest thy neighbor?" In condemning and censuring others, we are thrusting ourselves into God's seat, taking his scepter into our hands, and presuming to exercise one of his prerogatives.

Another reason for this command is that we cannot judge others justly and fairly. We have not sufficient knowledge of them. St. Paul says: "Judge nothing before the time, until the Lord come, who both will bring to light the hidden things of darkness, and make manifest the counsels of the hearts." Men's judgments cannot be aught but partial and superficial.

We do not know what may be the causes of the faults we would condemn in others. If we did we would be more charitable toward them. Some people's imperfections are an inheritance which they have received from their parents. They were born with the weaknesses that now mar their manhood. Or their faults have come through errors in their training and education. The nurse fell with the baby, and all down along the years the man goes about with a lameness or a deformity which mars his beauty of form. But he is not responsible for the marring, and criticism of the wounding in him would be cruel and unjust. There are hurts in character, woundings of the soul, which it is quite as unjust to condemn with anything but pity, for they are the inheritance of other men's wrong-doing.

There often are causes for the warpings and distortings of lives, which, if we understood them, would make us lenient to those about us and very patient with their peculiarities. We do not know what troubles people have, what secret sorrows, that so press upon their hearts as to affect their disposition, temper, or conduct. "If we could read the secret history of our enemies," says Longfellow, "we could find in each man's life sorrow and suffering enough to disarm all hostility." For example, we wonder at a man's want of cheerfulness. He seems unsocial, sour, cynical, cold. But all the while he is carrying a burden which almost crushes the life out of him. If we knew all that God knows of his life we would not speak a word of blame. Our censure would turn to pity and kindness, and we would silently try to help him bear his burden.

Our hearts are softened toward men when they are dead. We hush our fault-finding when we stand by a man's coffin. Commendation then takes the place of criticism. We see the life then in new light, which seems to emphasize whatever was beautiful in it, and into shadow whatever was unbeautiful. We are reverent toward the dead. Nothing but good should be spoken of them, we say. Death invests the life with sacredness in our eyes. It has gone to God. Yes, but is the life any the less sacred that moves before us or by our side, with all its sorrows and struggles and fears and hopes? We should be reverent toward the dead, speaking of them in hushed accents, but we should be no less reverent toward the living. Mary Mapes Dodge puts this thought in this striking way:—

> "'Speak tenderly! For he is dead,' we say;
> 'With gracious hand smooth all his roughened past,
> And fullest measure of reward forecast,
> Forgetting naught that glorified his brief day.'
> Yet when the brother, who, along our way,
> Prone with his burdens, heartworn in the strife,
> Totters before us—how we search his life!
> Censure and sternly punish while we may.
> Oh, weary are the paths of earth, and hard!
> And loving hearts alone are ours to guard.
> At least, begrudge not to the sore distraught
> The reverent silence of our pitying thought.
> Life, too, is sacred; and he best forgives
> Who say: 'He errs, but—tenderly! He lives.'"

A great deal of our judging of others is misjudging or unjust judging, because of the fragmentariness of our knowledge of their personal lives and experiences. It would ofttimes grieve us, and make us sorely ashamed of ourselves, if, when we have judged another severely, we should be shown a glimpse of the other's inner life, revealing hidden sorrows and struggles which are the cause of the things in him we have blamed so much. We have only a most partial view of another's life, and cannot form absolutely unerring judgments on what we see and know. We see only one side of an act, when there may be another side that altogether changes its quality. Whittier tells us of his pressed gentian, one side of which was but a blurred mass of crushed leaves, while the other showed all the exquisite beauty of the flower. Life is full of similar two-sided views of people and of acts. We see a man out in the world, and he appears harsh and stern. We see him some day at home where his invalid child lies and suffers, and there he is another man, kindly, thoughtful, with almost motherly gentleness. It would have been most unjust to this man if we had made up our judgment of him from the outside view alone, without seeing him in his child's sick-room.

A young man was severely criticized by his companions for his closeness and meanness. He received a good salary, but loved in a pinched way, without even the plain comforts that his friends thought he could easily have afforded, and without any of that generous expenditure in social ways in which other young men of his class indulged. Many strictures were made on his meanness — as it seemed to his companions. That was one side of his life; but there was another. That young man had an only sister — they were orphans — who was a great sufferer, shut in her room, kept on her bed continually. This only bother provided for her. That was the reason he lived so closely, saving every cent he could save, and doing without many things which other young men thought indispensable, that she in her loneliness and pain might be cared for and might have comforts. That was the other side of the character, the one side of which appeared so unattractive to his friends. We see how injust was their judgment, based on knowledge of only the one phase of his conduct. Seen in connection with its motive, the quality so severely censured became a mark of noble, manly beauty.

A tender story is told of Professor Blackie, of Edinburgh, which illustrates the same lesson. He was lecturing to a new class, and a student rose to read a paragraph, holding the book in his left hand. "Sir," thundered the professor, "hold your book in your right hand." The student attempted to speak. "No words, sir! your right hand, I say!" The lad held up his right arm, ending piteously at the wrist: "Sir, I hae nae right hand," he said.

Before the professor could open his lips there arose such a storm of hisses as one perhaps must go to Edinburgh to hear, and by it his voice was overborne. Then he left his place, and going down to the student he had unwittingly hurt, he put his arm around the lad's shoulders and drew him close to his breast. "My boy," said Blackie, — he now spoke very softly, yet not so softly but that every word was audible in the hush that had fallen on the classroom, — "You'll forgive me that I was overrough? I did not know — I did not know."

Our own imperfections also unfit us for judging fairly. With beams in our own eyes we cannot see clearly to pick motes out of our brother's eye. One of the qualities which make us incapable of impartial judgment of others is envy. There are few of us who can see our neighbor's life, work, and disposition without some warping and distortion of the picture. Envy has a strange effect on our moral vision. It shows the beautiful things in others with the beauty dimmed. It shows the blemishes and faults in them exaggerated. In other forms, too, the miserable selfishness of our hearts obtrudes itself and makes our judgments of others ofttimes really unkind and uncharitable. The lack of experience in struggle makes many people incapable of sympathy with sorely tempted ones. Those who have never known a care nor felt the pinching of want cannot understand the experiences of the poor. Thus, in very many ways, we are unfitted in ourselves to be judges of others.

Another reason why we should not judge others is that our business with them, our true duty toward them, is to help them to rise out of their faults. We are set together in life to make each other better. And the way to do this is not by prating continually about the faults we see in others. Nagging and scolding never yet made anybody saintly. Constant pointing out of blemishes never cured any one of his blemishes. Perhaps there is a duty of telling others of their faults; but, if so, it exists only in certain rare relations, and must be exercised only in a spirit of rare lovingness. We are often told that one of the finest qualities in a true friend is that he can and will faithfully tell us our faults. Perhaps that is true, but not many of us have grace enough to welcome and accept profitably such an office in a friend. A mother may tell her own children their faults, if she will do it wisely and affectionately, never in anger or impatience. A teacher may tell his pupils their mistakes and show them their faults, if it be done in true, loving desire for their improvement. But in ordinary friendship one cannot accept the office of censor, even when besought to do so, save with the strongest probability that the result will be the loss of the friendship, as the price paid for the possible curing of the friend's fault.

Nagging is not a means of grace. There is a more excellent way, the way of love. It is better, when we wish to correct faults in others, to be careful to let them see in us, in strong relief, the virtue, the excellence, opposite to the defect we see in them. It is the habit of a certain good man, if one of his family or friends mispronounces a word in his hearing, never pedantically to correct the error, but at some early opportunity to find occasion to use the same word, giving it the correct pronunciation. Something like this is wise in helping others out of their faults of character of conduct. An example is better than a criticism.

That was our Lord's way with his disciples. He never scolded them. He bore patiently with their dullness and slowness as scholars. He never wearied of repeating the same lesson over and over to them. But he was never censorious. Even he did not judge them. He did not keep telling them of all the blemishes he saw in them. That was not his way of seeking their growth into better, sweeter life. His heart was full of love. He saw back of all their infirmities and failures the sincerity and the desire to do right, and with infinite patience and gentleness he helped them ever toward the larger, better, sweeter life.

We need to relate ourselves to others as did Christ to his disciples, if we would help others to grow into spiritual beauty. Censoriousness accomplishes nothing in making people better. You can never make any one sweet by scolding him. Only gentleness will produce gentleness. Only love will cure infirmities of disposition. As a rule, fault-finding is exercised in any but a loving spirit. People are not truly grieved by the sins in others which they complacently expose and condemn. Too often they seem to delight in having discovered something not beautiful in a neighbor, and they swoop down upon the wrong thing like an unclean bird on carrion. If ever criticism is indulged in, it should be with deep grief for the friend, that the fault exists in him, and with sincere desire that for his sake it be removed; and then the criticism should be made, not in the ear of the world, but "between him and thee alone."

We should train ourselves, therefore, to see the good, not the evil, in others. We should speak approving words of what is beautiful in them, not bitter, condemning words of what may be imperfect or unlovely. We should look at others through eyes of love, not through eyes of envy or of selfishness, and should seek to heal with true affection's gentleness the things that are not as they should be.

> "How do we know what hearts have vilest sin?
> How do we know?
> Many, like sepulchers, are foul within,
> Whose outward garb is spotless as the snow;
> And many may be pure we think not so.
> How near to God the souls of such have been,
> What mercy secret penitence may win—
> How do we know?
>
> How can we tell who sinned more than we?
> How can we tell?
> We think our brother has walked guiltily,

Judging him in self-righteousness. Ah, well!
Perhaps, had we been driven through the hell
Of his untold temptations, we might be
Less upright in our daily walk than he—
How can we tell?

Dare we condemn the ills that others do?
Dare we condemn?
Their strength is small, their trails are not few;
The tide of wrong is difficult to stem.
And if to us more clearly then to them
Is given knowledge of the great and true,
More do they need our help and pity too—
Dare we condemn?

God help us all, and lead us day by day—
God help us all!
We cannot walk alone the perfect way.
Evil allures us, tempts us, and we fall;
We are but human, and our power is small;
Not one of us may boast, and not a day
Rolls o'er our heads but each hath need to say
God bless us all!"

Chapter 19

Christ's Withheld Lessons

"Is it true, O Christ in heaven,
That, whichever way we go,
Walls of darkness must surround us,
Things we would but cannot know?"

ALL learning is slow. This is true in proportion to the importance of the lessons. We learn some things quickly, but they are not the things which are of greatest value. Mere head-lessons are gotten more easily than heart lessons. We may memorize the beatitudes in a few minutes, but it takes many years to learn to live them. And in moral lessons this is the only learning that counts. Any one can get a code of ethics by heart, without much effort; but to get the faultless code wrought into conduct, disposition, spirit, character, is the work of a lifetime.

In life-teaching the lessons are given only as fast as they are learned. Our Master will not teach us more rapidly than we can take his lessons. It was in the midst of his most confidential talk with his disciples that he said he had many things to say to them which they could not ye bear. All wise teaching must be from the simplest rudiments up to the more complex knowledge. The mind is not capable of comprehending the higher elements till it has been developed and trained. Then truth itself is progressive, and the pupil is not prepared to receive the advanced lessons until he has mastered the rudiments.

Spiritual truths can be received only as we come to the experiences for which they are adapted. There are many of the divine promises which we can never claim, and whose blessedness we cannot realize, until we come to the points in life for which they were specially given. For example: "In the time of trouble he shall hide me in his pavilion." This word can mean nothing to the child playing amid the flowers, or to the young man or woman walking in sunny paths, without a care or a trial.

It can be understood only by one who is in trouble. Or, take Christ's word: "My grace is sufficient for thee." It was given first in place of an answer to a prayer for the removal of a sore trial. It meant divine strength to offset human weakness; and it cannot be received until there is a sense of need. Christ stands beside a happy young Christian and says, "I have a precious word to give you, one that shines with the beauty of divine love; but you cannot bear it yet." The disciple moves on along life's sunny path, and by and by comes into the shadows of sorrow of trouble. Again the Master stands beside him and says, "Now I can give you the word I withheld before. It is this: 'My grace is sufficient for thee.'" Then the promise glows with light and love.

There is a large part of the Bible which can be received by us only when we come into the places for which the words were given. There are promises for weakness which we can never get while we are strong. There are words for times of danger which we can never know in the days when we need no protection. There are consolations for sickness whose comfort we can never get while we are in robust health. There are promises for times of loneliness, when men walk in solitary ways, which never can come with real meaning to us while loving companions are by our side. There are words for old age which we never can appropriate for ourselves along the years of youth, when the arm is strong, the blood warm, and the heart brave. God cannot show us the stars while the sun shines in the heaven; and he cannot make known to us the precious things of love which he has prepared for our nights while it is yet day about us. Christ says to us then, "I have yet many things to say unto you, but ye cannot bear them now." We could not understand them. But by and by when we come into places of need, of sorrow, of weakness of human failure, of loneliness, of sickness, of old age, then he will tell us these other things, these long-withheld things, and they will be full of joy for our hearts. When night comes, he will show us the stars.

Older Christians will understand this. There are many things in the Bible which had little meaning for them in life's earlier day, but which one by one have shone out bright and beautiful along the years, as stars come out in the evening sky when the sun fades from the heavens. Even in childhood the words were said over and over; but they were repeated thoughtlessly because there had been no experience to prepare the heart to receive them. Then one day there crept a shadow over the life, and in the shadow the long familiar words began for the first time to have meaning. Other experiences of care, trial, and loss followed, and the precious words became more and more real. Now, in old age, as the sacred texts are repeated, they are the very rod and staff to the trembling, trusting spirit. No better illustration of this truth can be given than we have in the familiar lines which tell how as old hymn was learned: —

"Rock of Ages, cleft for me!"
Thoughtlessly the maiden sung;
Fell the words unconsciously
From her girlish, gleeful tongue;
Sang as little children sing;
Sang as sing the birds in June;
Fell the words like light leaves down
On the current of the tune—
"Rock of Ages, cleft for me,
Let me hide myself in thee!"

"Let me hide myself in thee!"
Felt her soul no need to hide —
Sweet the song as sweet could be,
And she had no thought beside;
All the words unheedingly
Fell from lips untouched by care,
Dreaming not that they might be
On some other lips a prayer—
"Rock of Ages, cleft for me,
Let me hide myself in thee!"

Rock of Ages, cleft for me!"
'Twas a woman sung them now,
Pleadingly and prayerfully.
Every word her heart did know;
Rose the song as storm-tossed bird
Beats with weary wing the air,
Every not with sorrow stirred,
Every syllable a prayer—
"Rock of Ages, cleft for me,
Let me hide myself in thee!"

"Rock of Ages, cleft for me!"
Lips grown aged sung the hymn,
Trustingly and tenderly,
Voice grown weak and eyes grown dim—
"Let me hide myself in thee!"
Trembling though the voice and low,

Ran the sweet strain peacefully,
Like a river in its flow;
Sang as only they can sing
Who life's thorny path have pressed;
Sang as only they can sing
Who behold the promised rest—
"Rock of Ages, cleft for me,
Let me hide myself in thee!"

"Rock of Ages, cleft for me!"
Sung above a coffin-lid—
Underneath, all restfully,
All life's joys and sorrows hid;
Nevermore, O storm-tossed soul,
Nevermore from wind and tide,
Nevermore from billows' roll,
Wilt thou need thyself to hide.
Could the sightless, sunken eyes
Closed beneath the soft gray hair;
Could the mute and stiffened lips
Move again in pleading prayer,
Still, aye still, the words would be,
"Let me hide myself in thee!"

Thus, as life goes on, the meaning of Christ's words come out clearer and clearer, until the child's heedless repetition of them becomes the utterance of the faith and trust of the strong man's very soul.

We cannot bear now the revealing of our own future. Christ knows it all. When a young Christian come to the Master's feet and says, "I will follow thee whithersoever thou leadest," the Master knows what that promise means. But he does not reveal the knowledge to his happy disciple. People sometimes say they wish they could look on into the years and see all that will come to them. But would this be a blessing? Would it make them happier? Could they shape their course better if they knew all that shall befall them, — the struggles, the victories, the defeats, the joys and sorrow, the failures of bright hopes, — just how long they will live?

Surely it is better we should not know our future. So the word of the Master is continually: "I have yet many things to say onto you but ye cannot bear them now." Only as we go on, step by step, does he disclose to us his will and plan for our life. Thus the joys of life do not dazzle us, for our hearts have been chastened so that we have learned how to receive them. The sorrows do not overwhelm us, because each one brings its own special comfort with it. But if we had known in advance the coming joys and prosperities, the exultation might have made us heedless of duty and of danger. We might have let go God's hand and have grown self-confident, thus missing the benediction that comes only to simple, trusting faith. If we had known of the struggles and trials before us, we might have become disheartened, thus failing of courage to endure. In either case we could not have borne the revealing, and it was in tenderness that the Master withheld it.

We could not bear the many things Christ has to tell us about heaven, therefore he does not tell them to us. The blessedness, if disclosed now, would dazzle and blind our eyes; the light must be let in upon us, little by little, so as not to harm us. Then if heaven were within our sight, as we toil and struggle and suffer here, the bliss would so excite us that we should be unfitted for duty. A traveler tells of returning to France after a long voyage to India. As soon as the sailors saw the shore of their own land they became incapable of attending to their duties on the ship. When they came into port and saw their friends on the quay, the excitement was so intense that another crew had to be found to take their place. Would it not be thus with us if heaven were visible from earth? Its blessedness would win us away from our duties. The sight of its splendors would so charm and entrance us that we should weary of earth's painful life. If we could see our loved ones on heaven's shore, we would not be content to stay here to finish our work. Surely it is better that more has not been revealed. The veiled glory does not dazzle us; and yet faith realizes it, and is sustained by the precious hope in its struggles in the night of earthly life, until at last the morning breaks.

This is the great law of divine revealing. We learn Christ's teaching as fast as we are able to bear it. So we may wait in patient faith when mysteries confront us, or when shadows lie on our pathway, confident that he who knows all has in gentle love withholden from us for the time the revealing we crave, because we could not yet endure the knowledge. Ever, therefore, our prayer may be:—

"Lead, kindly Light, amid th' encircling gloom,
Lead thou me on;
The night is dark, and I am far from home,
Lead thou me on.
Keep thou my feet; I do not ask to see
The distant scene: one step's enough for me."

Chapter 20

For the Days of Darkness

"Who followeth me shall walk in darkness never,
The light of life shall brighten all his way;
Nor things of time, nor things to come, shall sever
From him they love the children of the day."

We are not to anticipate trial. God wants us to take the days as they come, building little fences of trust about each one, shutting out all that does not belong to it. We are not to stain to-day's blue sky with to-morrow's clouds. We are not to burden to-day's strength with to-morrow's loads. We are not to walk sadly in bright youth, when we have no sorrows, because we know that later in life we must meet pain and grief. "Sufficient unto the day is the evil thereof." Yet we should live in the glad days so that when the bad days come they will not overwhelm us. For no matter how brightly the sun shines about us to-day, it will some time grow dark. No holy living, no kind of preparation beforehand, can keep the affliction away. That is not the way God blesses his children. There are ways of living in the sunny days so that when the night comes we shall not be left in utter darkness.

One way is by storing our minds with the promises of God. We may get a lesson right here from our geology. Ages ago vegetation grew rank and luxuriant. Wisely our earth piled away all the vast debris of the falling and decaying forests, and covered it up. It seemed a foolish sort of carefulness and economy. Of what use would all this mass of dead trees and vegetation ever be? But it is now earth's coalbeds, and it is lighting our homes in the dark night. In the days of human gladness, when there is no trouble, no pain, there are many of God's words which seem to have no meaning for us. We do not need them. They are for times of sorrow, and we have no sorrow. They are lamps for the darkness, and we are not walking in darkness. They are for days of pain and loss, and we have no pain, and are called to endure no loss. But if we are wise, if we would be ready for whatever the future may bring to us, we will not leave these unheeded words unappropriated. We will take them into our heart and fix them there, as one would fix lamps in a house during the daytime, to be ready to shine when night comes. Then when the sorrow comes, as it surely will come, we shall not be overtaken by the darkness. These promises for which we had no use in the days of human joy, but which we took into our heart against the time of need, will now shine down upon us and fill our gloom with sweet light from heaven. That is one way of walking while we have the light, so that the darkness will not overtake us and overwhelm us. Hang the lamps all about your heart's chambers during the day.

Another way is by keeping the vision clear all the time between our souls and heaven. It is not easy in the time of unbroken worldly prosperity to maintain unbroken communion with God. Prosperity fosters many things that serve to cut of our spiritual outlook. A man built a house on a spot which commanded a beautiful view of distant mountains and a great stretch of sky. Then he said, "I must have trees to shelter the house. Trees make any place more lovely." So he planted a number of fine trees, and they grew up, and were much admired. But the trees were close together, and, as they grew, their branches interlaced; and by and by they shut out the distant view, so that the mountains were no longer visible from the house, and scarcely a glimpse could be had of the sky.

So it is often with men's lives. In their prosperity men gather about them many earthly interests and pleasures. These are very sweet; but sometimes they shut out the view of heaven's glorious mountains, and of the blessed spiritual things which are the realities of Christian faith. Many a life thus loses its familiarity with Christ, and the invisible things of God become less and less clear to the vision. Earthly interests absorb the thought and the affections. Then when sorrow comes and it grows dark, the heart cannot find its refuge, and goes uncomforted. The familiar joys have lost their power to bless, and the soul has no experience of the higher joys.

Walk while ye have lights, that the darkness overtake you not, swallow you not up. That is, in the days of earthly joy and prosperity, keep the view between your soul and heaven clear and open. Do not let the trees grow up about your life's home, so as to shut out your view of the mountains of God. Keep on intimate and familiar terms all the time with Christ. Then when night comes the lights from your Father's house will shine down upon your darkness. Bereft of human companionship, the consciousness of the presence, the companionship, and the love of Jesus Christ, your unseen Friend, will become more and more real to you. Thus walking while you have the lights, the darkness when it comes will not overwhelm you.

There are many such experiences of sorrow. They come, perhaps suddenly, to some Christian who has known only gladness before; but the life is not crushed. In the darkness the face of Christ appears in beauty never seen before, and the sad heart is comforted.

Still another way in which we may be prepared in the light for the darkness is suggested by our Lord himself in one of his teachings. "While ye have the light, believe on the light, that ye may become sons of light." There is something very beautiful in this. If you walk in the light, the light will enter into you, and you will become a son of light. If a diamond lie for a while in the sunshine, and then be carried into a darkened room, a soft light will pour out from it. We know how it was with John, for example. He walked in the light of Christ for three years, and the light entered into him, into his very soul, until he became a shining light. So it was with all who were close friends of Christ.

And we may walk in the light of Christ just as truly as did those who knew him in the flesh. Christ is not behind us, a mere historical figure of long centuries past. He is with us, as really present by our side as he was by Mary when she sat at his feet, or by John when he lay upon that blessed bosom. So we can walk in the light of Christ; and as we do so, we shall become light ourselves, filled with his light.

But how can we get the light into our own life? Only by opening our heart to the love of Christ. There were a great many people in those ancient days who saw Jesus, who met him ofttimes, who heard his wonderful word, who beheld his sweet life, who were witnesses of his patience, his gentleness, his gracious kindness, his unselfish ministry, but who never became children of light. Their lives remained dull and cold and dark as though they had never seen him. On the other hand, there were a few people who walked in the light of Christ, and became themselves transfigured, bright, shining children of light.

What was the curse of this difference in the influence of Jesus upon different lives? It is very plain to one who understands the law of spiritual impression. The people at large saw Christ, heard his words, beheld his sweet life, walked beneath his influence, but kept their hearts shut against him. Christ's life flowed all about them, but found no entrance into them. The friends of Christ, however, believed in him, loved him, opened their souls to him, came into intimate communion with him, received his words, let his Spirit pour into their hearts. The divine life that flowed about them filled them. There is the same difference always among those who live under the influence of Christ. Not all take the blessing into their souls. Thousands know the truth of Christianity who have not received the spirit of Christianity. But those who receive Christ himself become Christians, Christ's men, children of light, and shine themselves with the same light.

That is what our Lord means for us when he says, "Ye are the light of the world." We are lighted at the flame of his life. Then as he was in the world so are we in the world. Our lives shine too. In our little measure we become Christs to others. We, in turn, are comforters of the sorrow of the sorrowing, inspirers of hope in the despairing, and of strength in the weak. There is no other secret in the art of comfort. There is no use in your saying over verses of Scripture to those who are in darkness of trouble, if that is all you do. You must have light in yourself. The sorrowing must hear the heart-beat in your words. The life of Christ must flow through your lips and shine in your face. Walk in the light until you became a child of light, and then you can go out to shine for Christ in the world.

If we are children of light, no darkness can overwhelm us. Night does not quench the lights that shine in our streets and in our homes; they appear only the brighter as the darkness deepens. So, if we are children of light, the darkness of sorrow falling about us will not overwhelm us. It will not be dark in our soul, however deep the gloom outside. In the time of the three days' darkness in Egypt, God's people had light in their houses. Thus it is in the Christian home in the time of sorest and most sudden sorrow. This is the secret of comfort. Be filled with Christ. Open your heart to his love, to his Spirit, to his peace, to his joy, to his life. Abide in Christ until Christ abides in you, until you are filled with all the fullness of God. Then you need not fear any sorrow, for the comfort is in yourself. No darkness can make it dark in your soul, because the light of Christ shines there.

Then in your own sorrow you will be a comforter of others. Jesus, in his darkest hours, forget himself and sought to comfort others. On the night of his betrayal, when the shadows were deepening about him, he took the disciples into the upper room, and comforted them in their deep and bitter grief with the most precious words of comfort earth's sorrowing ones have ever heard. Let those who are themselves crying out for consolation, go out into the sad world, and forget their won affliction as they seek to lift up other mourners. The words Christ has spoken to them in their hour of darkness let them speak forth again. Let the mother wither with the empty crib and the empty bosom go to the home where white crape hangs on the door, put her are around the mother who sits there in her bitter grief, and tell her she understands the pain of her heart, and then whisper to her the comfort of God's love. In trying to console others, the mourner will find consolation for herself.

There is no other secret of comfort like this. Walk in the light while ye have the lights, and ye shall become the children of light. Then no darkness can overtake you, or quench the light that shines in you. Then you will be a light in the world to brighten other lives in their sorrow. Of a great preacher a poet wrote:—

> "Where he trod,
> Love of God
> Blossomed into sight.
> Form and hue
> Lovelier grew
> In the eternal light."

Chapter 21

Hidden Words in the Bible

"More and more stars! And ever as I gaze
Brighter and brighter seen!
Whence come they, Father? Trace me out their ways
Far in the deep serene."
~Keble.

There is a great deal of beauty in the world which lies too deep for our eyes. There are millions of stars in depths of the heavens which no telescope reveals. Night unveils to us splendors which lie hidden in day's glare.

One may write with invisible ink, and the words fade out after the pen, leaving no trace. Yet they remain in the paper, hidden there, unseen and unsuspected by any eye that scans it. But if one day the paper be exposed to heat, the hidden words come out in all clearness, every line appearing in distinctness.

There is a sense in which the revealings of God in the Bible are hidden. They are not hidden because God seeks to keep them from us, but because we must be brought into a certain condition before we can receive them. One said the other day, "Why did I never see the rich meaning of that psalm before?" We had been going over one of the psalms together, as I sat at my friend's bedside, and we had seen many sweet things in some of the verses. My friend almost chided herself with dullness of vision, or with carelessness in reading, in not having seen the precious meanings before. "I have read that psalm hundreds of times," she said. "These sweet thoughts were lying in the verses all the while, but I never saw them until now. Why was it? Did God mean to hide them from me?"

The answer to these questions is that the revealings are made and the blessings bestowed really at the earliest possible moment. The stars are in the sky all day, but we cannot behold them until night comes. My friend could not have seen the precious thought in the psalm six months before. Then she was in health, active, swift in movement, strong, with no consciousness of weakness, rich in human hopes and expectations. And she found very many precious things then in the Bible. It had its lessons, its encouragements, its interpretations. Just what she needed and craved in those active days the book had for her. But the particular revealings which she gets now from its words she did not then find. Now she needs comfort for weakness; strength to endure pain patiently; grace to enable her to readjust her life to its new conditions, assurance of divine love and care in her experience of feebleness. She did not need these special revealings in the time of health and activity, and they were not then available to her.

The experience is a very common one. A happy young girl may sing sweetly the hymn,-

> "Jesus lover of my soul,
> Let me to thy bosom fly;"

And yet it may mean almost nothing to her. She feels no need to fly to the divine bosom. She is conscious of no danger, of no enemy pursuing, of no storm gathering. The words ripple from her tongue in musical measure and tone, but there really is no experience in her heart to interpret them to her. A few years later she is a woman, with many cares, burdens, trials, and sorrows, and again she sings the song:—

> "Jesus, lover of my soul,
> Let me to thy bosom fly;
> While the nearer waters roll,
> While the tempest still is high:
> Hide me, O my Saviour, hide,
> Till the storm of life is past;
> Safe into the haven guide,
> Oh, receive my soul at last."

And now she feels word as it drops from her lips in pleading accents. Every syllable is now a prayer from her heart. On the wings of her song her heart rises,—

> "As storm-tossed bird
> Beats with weary wing the air."

What makes the song such a new song to her? New experiences have come into her life, and amid these she has learned her own insufficiency and her need of divine shelter, and has learned also of the preciousness of the refuge in the bosom of Christ.

The same is true of very many divine comforts. There are Bible texts which open to the young. They read the sacred book in the bright years when there is no care, no sense of weakness, no consciousness of need, and many of its words speak to them in thoughts of gladness and cheer. Meanwhile there are other words that read sweetly enough, yet over which they do not linger, out of which comes to their heart no soothing voice. Then they go on for a few years, and at length the way slopes into gloom. A child is sick, and the strong man is watching beside its bed, with heart burdened and anxious. Or he is brought down himself to a sickbed, where he has time for thought. He knows his illness is serious, — that he may never recover. Now he is ready for some new Bible verses. He needs some of the comfort that thus far has been hidden from him in the words of God, whose deeper meaning he could not receive until now. For example, there are the opening lines of the Forty-sixth Psalm:—

"God is our refuge and strength,
A very present help in trouble."

He felt no need of a refuge in the sunny days, and never availed himself of it. Indeed, the door did not seem to open to him at all. But now in his weakness and fear he seeks a refuge, some place to hide; and, coming upon this word of God, it opens at once to him, and he runs into it and finds warmth, shelter, love, safety, all within its gate.

He had not felt the need of God's help and companionship when human friendship seemed so all-sufficient, and the word about "a very present help in trouble" had no personal meaning for him then; now, however, the human friendship, sweet as they are, are inadequate, or they are far away. In this condition the assurance that God is "a very present help" is a blessed revealing, and it is the opening to him of a new secret of blessing. When he knows this all the way of life seems lighted with a new and strange illumining. He fears no dangers, no trials, no battles, for with God for a very present help, he can never fail nor falter.

It is thus that all the Bible words must be gotten. There are many precious promises for those who are tempted; but until you are in the grip of temptation you cannot draw the blessing from the quiver which God binds on his tempted ones. There are tender and precious words for the widow; but while the beloved wife has

her husband by her side, strong, brave and true, these words are
yet closed storehouses to her. They can become hers only when
she wears the badge of widowhood, and sits lonely by the coffin of
her dead, or amid the cares and burdens which her bereavement
has cast at her feet. There are sweet words for orphan children;
but while the children have both father and mother with them,
and are swelling in the shelter of a happy home, they cannot draw
upon this reserve of divine goodness. Only when they have lost
one or other or both parents can they have lost one or other or
both parents can they quote such a Bible promise as this:—

> "When my father and my mother forsake me,
> Then the Lord will take me up."

There are very loving promises, too, for the old; but the man or
woman in youth or mid-life cannot take them. There are beatitudes
for certain conditions. "Blessed are they that mourn; for they shall
be comforted." But only those who are in sorrow can experience
the blessedness of divine comfort." It never can be learned while
the heart knows not grief. Another beatitude is: "Blessed are they
which do hunger and thirst after righteousness; for they shall be
filled." But there must first be hunger and thirst before there can
be heart-filling.

Thus all the Bible treasures are ready to open to us the moment
we have the experience which the particular grace in them is intended to supply. Hence it is that the Bible is never exhausted. Men
read it over and over again, and each time they find something new
in it, — new promises, new comforts, new revealings of love. The
reason is, they are growing in experience, and every new experience
develops new needs, and brings them to new revealings.

Another feature of this truth is that the revealings are made only
as we enter upon the needs. The blessing for each day is locked up
in the little circle of that day, and we cannot even get to it until we
come to the place. But when the need comes, the supple is always
ready. George MacDonald puts this truth in a sentence: "As you
grow ready for it, somewhere or other you will find what is needful
for you, in a book or a friend." Nor is it mere chance that brings
the supply, the help, the light, thus, just at the right moment. The
hand of God guides all such chances. It is divine thoughtfulness
that watches and always has the goodness ready at the instant of
want. As the nature awakes, and its needs begin to express themselves in hungerings and cravings, God brings to us in his own

way that which our newly awakened craving requires. He watches us, and at the right moment has ready the blessing for the moment.

Every new providence which opens before us has in its own little circle its own supply if goodness. Take, again, for illustration, the case of the young friend who was sick. She had never been ill before. When the sickness came on, the experience was altogether new and strange. At first it seemed mysterious to her, and she was alarmed; but soon she began to realize what while the experience was new and painful, she was receiving new blessings, had come upon new revealings of God's goodness. For one thing, she had never before experienced such tenderness of love in her own home as now came to her from all her loved ones. The whole household life began to turn about her sick-room. The love was all there before in the hearts of father, mother, sister, brother, — they loved her no more than before; but in her happiness and health the love had never shown itself as it did now when she lay among the pillows, white and weak and suffering. Now each vied with all the others in the expression of kindly interest.

Then, never had she known before that she had so many friends outside her home. There had always been kindness and courtesy, but now there seemed hundred who wanted to show their love in some tender way. Still another new blessing that opened to her in her sickness was her Bible. She had always been a Bible reader, and the book has meant much to her in the bright, sunny days of life. But now she found precious love-thoughts, shining like diamonds, in words which had meant but little to her before. Nor was that all; she found revealings of the love of God which she had never experienced in her days of strength. The friendship of Christ never before had seemed so close and real as it now became. Thus the providence of God which had brought her into a darkened sick-room, had brought her also to a new unfolding of divine goodness, to which she could not have come had not the illness been experience.

So it is continually in life. The things we dread — the losses, the sorrows, the adversities — bring us to new goodness and blessing which we should have missed if the painful trial had not come. Close beside the bitter fountain of Marah grew the tree that sweetened the water. Hard by every sorrow waits the comfort needed to alleviate it. Every loss has wrapped up in it some compensating gain. It is in human weakness that God's strength is made perfect.

We may set it down as a principle, a law of Christ's kingdom,

which has no exceptions, that for every new condition or experience in any Christian life, there is a special reserve of divine goodness, whose supply will adequately meet all the needs of the hour.
We need never fear, therefore, that we shall be led to any place in
which we cannot have grace to live sweetly and faithfully. "As thy
days, so shall thy strength be," is the unfailing divine promise. But
the grace is hidden in the need, and cannot be gotten in advance.
The grace for sorrow cannot be given when we are in joy. The grace
for dying we cannot get when we are in the midst of life's duties.
And surely that is not the help we need then, but, rather, wisdom
and strength to live nobly, lovingly, truly. Then when we approach
death we shall be sustained and led through the valley into life.

Chapter 22

Getting the Joy of Christ

"Take Joy home,
And make a place in thy great heart for her,
And give her time to grow, and cherish her!
Then will she come and often sing to thee
When thou art working in the furrows! ay,
Or weeding in the sacred hours of dawn.
It is a comely fashion to be glad—
Joy is the grace we say to God."
~Jean Ingelow.

The ideal life is one of joy. The face ought to be shining, — shining even in darkness. People say this is a sad world. Yes, for those who have eyes only for shadows. What we see is the imaging on the life around us of the colors of our own inner life. He who has the bird in his eyes sees the bird in the bush. He who has songs in his heart hears songs wherever he goes. This is a sad world for the sad man. Darkness within finds only darkness without. But if one carries a lantern when he goes out at night, one finds light wherever he goes. If one's face shines with an inner joy, one finds joy even in the deep night of sorrow.

Christ said a great deal about desiring joy in his disciples. He put it both in sermon and in prayer. He said he had spoken to them certain things in order that they might have his joy in them. It is clear that joy was his ideal for Christian life.

It is remarkable, too, that most of his words about joy were spoken the night before he died. This suggests that he meant his followers to have this joy, not only in their happy days, but when they were in sadness. It is evident, also, that it is not earthly gladness that he desires his friends to have, but a joy that dwells deep in the heart, — too deep for any earthly pain or sorrow to touch.

Surely here is a secret worth learning. There are a thousand things in this world that tend to disturb or destroy human happiness. If there is a way to live beyond the reach of these things, to live a life calm, serene, rejoicing, victorious, songful, in the midst of sorrow, loss, struggle, pain, and wrong, we ought to know it.

It is certain that we cannot get this joy by finding a place where the world's cares and hurts cannot reach us. There is no such place on this earth. No walls can shut out pain and travail. Christ did not ask that his disciples should be taken out of the world. They must live, as he did, in ordinary human condition. The wind blows no more softly for you because you are God's child. Christ does not give us his joy by sheltering us from the things that might disturb the joy.

Nor does he give it by so changing our nature that we shall not feel the griefs and pains of life. To do this he would have to rob our hearts of the very qualities in them that are noblest and divinest. Powers to enjoy and to be happy would also be destroyed with the power to suffer; for our joys and pains grow on the same stalk. Rack, stocks, and prison chains hurt the disciples no less because they had the love of Christ in them.

We must get Christ's joy as he got it. One secret was his unbroken consciousness of his Father's love. When men hated him, when the world assaulted him, he fled to his Father, and found a refuge into which none could follow him, whose calm peace none could disturb. We, too, must keep ourselves in the love of God if we would find this joy.

Absolute devotion to the divine will was another of the secrets of Christ's joy. He never did his own will. In this way only can we find joy. "True, pure joy," says Amiel, "consists in the union of the individual will with the divine will, and in the faith that this supreme will is directed by love."

Another secret of the joy of Christ was in his service and sacrifice of love. The angels see human joy on earth, not where men seek for happiness of their own, not where they are loving to find their own good and pleasure, but where they are toiling and denying themselves to give happiness to others. Christ's whole life was dsvoted to ministry for others, and every service of love yielded him joy. His death, too, was the voluntary giving of himself for others. There is a beautiful legend which gives us a glimpse of the joy which Christ found even in going to his cross. Father Ryan gives it thus,—

> "He walked beside the sea: he took his sandals off
> To bathe his wary feet in the pure, cool wave,—
> For he had walked across the desert sands

All day long,—and as he bathed his feet,
He murmured to himself, 'Three years! Three years!
And then, poor feet, the cruel nails will come
And make you bleed; but that blood will lave
All weary feet on all their thorny ways.'"

The deepest joy Christ's life must have been in his dying, for this was his greatest sacrifice and service. We get a glimmering of this experience in the word which says that "for the joy set before him he endured the cross, despising the shame;" and we have its foreshadowing in the prophetic assurance that he should see of the travial of his soul, and should be satisfied. We can get this joy of Christ only as we enter into his life of selfgiving love. Selfishness yields no true gladness. Serving starts songs in the heart. If we would have the joy of Christ we must enter into the spirit of the life of Christ. He was in this world to bless and save it. We can share his joy only as few share his love for the world, and love to bless and help to save it.

Another secret of the joy of Christ was in his always keeping his face toward the light. His look was ever upward. His eye was ever turned toward his Father and toward heaven. He saw only brightness. Many Christians need to learn this lesson. They look too much at the darkness of the world. They think of their sorrow, not of their joy. They let fear drive out courage and hope. If we would have Christ's joy we must train ourselves persistently — it is matter of training and habit largely — to look toward the light. There are flowers that keep their faces always turned toward the sun. That is the way we should learn to live. If we look ever toward the light, the light will enter into us and fill us with its own radiance.

In another of our Lord's words he tells us that Christian joy is transformed sorrow. He said to his disciples, "Your sorrow shall be turned into joy." He did not tell them that their sorrow should be taken away and joy given in its place, but that the sorrow itself should be turned into joy. When there has been a bereavement, he does not comfort by giving back the loved one. When there has been a disappointment, he does not undo it, and put into the life the dear thing that was wanted so much. The trouble is not removed, but it becomes a joy. This was fulfilled literally in respect to the cross, whose utter blackness became, later, the most glorious light the world has ever seen.

The same transformation takes place in every sorrow of Christian faith; it is turned into joy. In the depths of every dark thundercloud there is a rainbow hidden, which will break forth when the sun smites upon the cloud. And there is no trouble that comes to any Christian which has not, lying concealed within its folds, a divine blessing of joy, which will be revealed when the love of Christ shines upon it. You bow low in sorrow then death has touched a loved one of yours and the circle is broken. The loss seems irreparable. The grief appears too deep ever to receive comfort. But the Comforter comes, the consolations of divine love are given, and the sorrow is turned into joy. The sense of loss is not taken away. The friend is not given back. The keenness of the grief is not softened. But the love of Christ is revealed. The truth of immortal blessedness becomes a window through which faith's eyes sees into the heavenly glory, beholding, not death, but radiant life. The will of God, that seemed to crush like a falling avalanche the heart's frail joys, appears not the very hand of love, blessing, and doing good. The sorrow becomes deep joy.

In every life that has passed through such experiences and has kept its faith, the sweetest, richest joys are always transformed sorrow. The best things in any life are not things born of summer days, the things that come without cost or effort. One writes:—

"Joys that cost nothing give us little pleasure;
We value most the things most hardly won.
Men that delve deep to find earth's hidden treasure
Would pass it by if open to the sun."

The things we prize most are not those we have gathered, as one plucks flowers on a summer hillside, from the gardens of ease and worldly pleasure. They are things that have become ours through pain, struggle, self-denial, and tears. The lessons learned with greatest difficulty are the ones that are most to us in value and profit. Out of the hardest experiences of struggle and sacrifice we get the qualities that are the brightest ornaments of our character, and the noblest elements of our strength. The lenses through which now we see deepest into heaven once were salt tears. The treasures we hold now with firmest clasp once seemed marred things, unsightly unlovely, things we shrank from receiving. The points in our past which now appear to have been fullest of outcome of good for our life, are those which at the time seemed God's strange ways with us. Christian joy is transformed sorrow.

Another thing about this joy that Christ gives is that it cannot be taken away from us. Not dependent on earthly conditions, earthly accidents cannot reach it. Very much of our happiness others can take from us. They may smite us with bodily wounding. We may lose out of our own life the things we love, the things which give us comfort and pleasure. But, if we are believers in Christ, we have an inner gladness which no one can touch.

We can conceive of a strong fortress, in time of war, all of whose outer approaches may be assailed and despoiled, but within whose walls and gates there is a place of security which no enemy can enter, which no desolating hand of war can touch. There, if you were to pass within, you would find a quiet home, with music and pictures, with garden and flowers, with love and peace. Like this is the true Christian life. It has its unassailable fortress. Without in the world there are troubles and antagonisms, and the other gladness may all be swept away; but, within, there is a holy place of peace with nothing can invade. How that man is to be pitied who has no joy that others cannot take away, whose whole life, to its innermost stronghold, is open to the tread of alien feet! It is dreadful to have no joys of which the world cannot rob us, to have all our happiness, the deepest and most sacred, within the reach of human or earthly despoiling. Yet there are many people of whom this is true. They have no inner sanctuary of life which is beyond the reach of intrusion, which no foot can invade, which no hand can desecrate. But if we are the friends of Christ, our heart's joy should be inviolable. Our property, our loved ones, our health, may be taken away, and all earthly sources of happiness despoiled; but deep within, untouched and untouchable, the joy of Christ should still and ever abide.

This is the ideal Christian life. It is possible to every one, — the weakest, the most exposed, the sorely troubled, — possible, but possible only in Christ. There is no self-sufficiency in us which will give it to us. The dream of self-culture may be most radiant, but it is only a dream; it never can be realized. All that self alone can build up may be destroyed. The fairy palace of self-sufficiency which one may pile up can be nothing more than a house built upon the sand, which the floods will sweep away. But when we have Christ in our heart, we have a life which no one can touch, whose joy lives on, sweet, calm, and serene amid all earth's strifes and trial.

This is the life every one should seek to live. We should not carry our joy where every earthly experience can destroy it, but only where it will be safe from whatsoever might quench it. It is impossible to estimate the power for good, in this sad, struggling life, of a bright, glad, shining face.

> "Of all the lights you carry in your face,
> Joy shines farthest out to sea."

One of the best things any of us can do for this world is to show it ever a victorious life of joy, a face that shines even through tears, a beauty of the Lord which glows with radiance even in the night. That is the life the Master wants every follower of his to live; and we can live it, too, if our life is truly hid with Christ in God.

Chapter 23

The Need of the Afterlook

"And one can well afford to wait a season,
Till all that is dark shall be made bright,
If not with earthly, then with heavenly light,
And we shall came at least to know the reason
Of all the toil, the seeming loss, the pain."

THERE are many things in this world which we cannot understand. At its furthest reach our human knowledge only skirts the outermost edge of what is known to Omniscience. We soon realize this when we begin the study of any science. We learn a few facts, and few principles, pressing a little way into our subject, and then we become aware that there is a vast region beyond us into which we cannot enter. The philosopher's illustration is always true, — at the best we are only children, standing by the shore of a great sea, picking up here and there a brilliant shell or a polished pebble, while the deep sea lies beyond our reach, filled with far more brilliant things than those we have found.

This is not surprising when we consider our own finiteness and the narrow limitations of our powers, and the infinity of God, and the vastness of his universe. After we have studied the divine works and ways to the very uttermost of our power to understand, we can only say with Job,—

"Lo, these are but the outskirts of his ways,
And how small a whisper do we hear of him!
But the thunder of his power who can understand?"

A great English preacher illustrates the littleness, the fragmentariness, and the imperfectness of human knowledge of God's works, by the case of a fly crawling upon one of the pillars of St. Paul's Cathedral. What does the fly know of the architect's magnificent design in that great building? It sees only the little space of stone on which it moves; and the carving and mountains cutting off its progress and obscuring its view. So is the wisest man in the midst of the vast universe of God. He can see only for a little space about him. He can perceive but a little glimmer of the divine meaning in the things he sees. He can have but the dimmest, faintest conception of the wonderful plan of God which takes in all worlds, all human lives, and all ages.

We cannot expect to know all God's thoughts; we should have to be equal to him in wisdom to do this. A god whom we could fully understand, and in whose words and workings we should find no mystery, could not be God to us. We cannot expect to know God's design in the providences that touch human affairs and affect our own lives. We cannot trace the results of his acts through centuries to come, to know what the final outcome of them will be. We cannot tell what beautiful trees, with full, rich fruitage, will grow from the rough, dark seeds which to-day the Master plants in our life-garden. We cannot tell what blessing will come in the long future from the sorrow that now lays its heavy hand upon us.

When we begin to read a tale written by some great author, we cannot tell from the opening chapters what the outcome of the story will be. Nor can we know what will be the last chapters of any story of providence beginning to-day in our life or in our home, perhaps in a way that seems dark and sad. For example, the first chapters of the story of Joseph's life appeared very hopeless. He was torn away from his home. He was sold as a slave, and carried to a heathen country. There we soon find him in prison on false charges. Dark providences dimmed the opening morning of this young man's life. But we know how splendidly the story ends. So it has been in countless other life narratives.

There is a story of a certain rabbi who entered a town and met a little maid carrying in her hand a basket which was closely covered. "Tell me, my good child," said the rabbi, "what you have in that basket." The child answered modestly, "If my mother had wished that any one should know the contents of this basket, she would not have covered it." God covers up many things from our eyes. Some of these he desires us to search out for ourselves. Men are continually thinking over God's thoughts, reading the lines of God's writing in his word and works. But there are many things in the realm of God's providence which we cannot know. The future is yet beyond our ken, and it is foolish and wrong for us to vex ourselves with trying to find out what it has in store. If God had meant us to know what the coming years have for us, he would not have covered them up as he has done. We know one thing, — that he in whose hands are the future events of our lives is good and living, that he is our wisest and best Friend. Instead of knowing, we may trust. There is a secret of confidence in our Master's words, "What I do thou knowest not now." We know the character of him in whose hand are all the affairs of our lives. His name is love. We need never fear that what he does can be either mistaken or unkind. "What I do " written on any cup that is put to our lips ought to be assurance enough that there is a blessing in the cup for us.

> "I will say it over and over, this and every day:
> Whatsoever the Master orders, come what may,
> It is the Lord's appointment;
> For only his love can see
> What is wisest, best, and right,
> What is truly good for me."

But there is yet another word in our Master's saying which is a window of heaven, letting in bright light. "Thou knowest not now," he says. The emphatic "now" tells us that the veiling is but for a time. This is confirmed by the assurance which he hastens to give: "but thou shalt understand hereafter." There are many things in our lives that we cannot understand until hereafter. There are many things which cannot be made clear to us until we have larger knowledge of ourselves. Many of the mysteries of childhood are open as day to manhood. There are certain things that can be made known to us only at certain stages of personal experience. We cannot see the stars until night comes; there are revealings of blessing which never can be ours until we enter life's shadow. Then there are things which cannot yet be understood because they are unfinished works. There are things that can be wrought out only slowly and through processes which require ofttimes long years of time. No artist will permit any one to judge of his picture while it is incomplete; in the preliminary stages of his work it gives no true and adequate revealing of its final beauty. Many of the providences of our lives appear at first mysterious, because they are but the beginning of the outworking of thoughts of divine love. Some day when they are wrought out in completeness they will be beautiful and good as are all God's finished works. "Thou shalt understand hereafter."

Some of these dark things we may see made plain in this world. Jacob lived to understand the strange providence which took Joseph away from him. Joseph lived to understand what the Lord was doing with him in his youth when he allowed him to be so

cruelly dealt with. The disciples of Christ lived to understand the
dark enigma of their Master's life which so perplexed them, — the
mystery of the rejected, suffering, dying Messiah. Many people live
to see in their after-years an outcome of beauty and blessing in
experiences which, when they first entered them, appeared only
dark and destructive. The old man sitting in the quiet of life's evening sees bright rainbows in the very bosom of the clouds now re-
ceding, which, when they were passing over his head, were black
with tempest.

One writes of two views of life; first, of life as it appears to childhood, and then as it looks to old age. The child has not yet come
up to the perplexities of human experience.

> "Sweet face of childhood—
> thou lookest out on life with trusting eyes,
> Unknowing yet the awful mysteries
> Of sin and sorrow, want and grief and pain;
> For thine is perfect innocence.
> Yet some day thou shalt know the pain of life,
> And all its stern and hard realities.
> God shield thee when that searching day shall come!"

The old man has passed through all the mystery of life's trial,
and sees now the finished work, the results of discipline, the gold
purified and minted.

> "Sweet face of age—
> Thou lookest out on life full trustingly;
> Yet thou hast known the darkest mysteries
> Which compass and ensnare the souls of men,
> For thou regardest all the woes of life
> As but blows which call the statue forth
> From out the marble; thou hast learned
> That fire consumes the dross, refines the gold;
> And thou hast found at last behind it all
> Infinite love and wisdom infinite,
> Till now thou standest face to face with God."

Thus, much of the mystery of providence becomes clear even in
the present life. We have only to be patient and wait a little while
to see the unveilings of the completed work, the coming to sweet
and mellow ripeness of the fruit that seemed better at the first, the
working out in blessed beauty of the dark enigma of providence

which so perplexed us.

But there are other cases in which the explanation is not made in this world. Human life is too short for the finishing of all the work of divine love which begins in darkness. If life ended at the grave, we might not be able at all times to say that God is just and equal in his dealings with men. Some good people's lives seem to be all darkness and trial, with no explanation, no revealing of good. There are wrongs not righted here. There are good men misunderstood, maligned, misrepresented, bearing the odium of false accusation, suffering for the sins of others, and waiting all their years for vindication which comes not, at last dying with the shadow upon their name. If there were no life beyond death we could not always say that God's ways are equal.

But life goes on, on the other side of the grave, and there will be time enough there for the fullest outworking of all earth's unfinished providences. All wrongs will there be righted and all perplexities solved. The shadows of injustice that have hung over good men in this world will vanish, and the names bearing reproach here without cause will shine forth like the stars. "What I do thou knowest not now, but thou shalt understand hereafter."